What people are saying about ...

MW01040290

Flash Theology

"'The more you know God personally, the more you can enjoy and appreciate him for who he is.' That's the purpose of *Flash Theology*, and that's the foundational purpose behind *The Chosen*, which is why I'm so excited about this vital book. Reading it will help you know God more personally. What's better than that?"

Dallas Jenkins, creator of *The Chosen*

"*Flash Theology* is a fun, easy-to-digest book on basic Christian theology that is both instructional and inspiring. It is a great resource for anyone who wants to know and understand our Creator better."

Zach Terry, president of Maximum Life, Inc., and author of *Our Fight*

"*Flash Theology* is a visually stunning and innovative approach to learning systematic theology. The visual illustrations bring to life theologically complex ideas in an accessible way for every student of the Bible. My favorite part of Jenny and Brayden's approach is how easily this can be used for personal devotions."

Joel Muddamalle, PhD, director of theology and research at Proverbs 31 Ministries

"If you've ever wrestled with your faith, found the Bible hard to understand, or hit an impasse between reality and theology, this book invites you to rediscover God's grand plan for the world and for you. Every Christ follower needs to rest a moment in the timeless truths presented in this book!"

Erica Wiggenhorn, founder of Every Life Ministries, international speaker, and multipublished author, including *Unexplainable Jesus*

"Whether you've walked with God your whole life or are just beginning to explore the mystery of God's love, this book will meet you right where you are and fuel your faith. *Flash Theology* helps peel back the veil that complicates our ability to know God by offering rock-solid truths with engaging visuals and clear explanations. Are you ready to dive in and know the triune God more? Get ready to dive deep! The invitation to a richer relationship with God in these pages is going to flood you with a greater understanding of how incredible the living God is and how incredibly LOVED you are!"

Kellie Haddock, hope giver and singer-songwriter

"Bite-sized and visually delicious. I love how this book takes huge concepts about God and makes them accessible to regular people. It will help you see and love him more!"

Justin Whitmel Earley, lawyer, speaker, and author of *The Common Rule* and *Habits of the Household*

"*Flash Theology* is not just for theologians, but it is for every person who longs to understand the divine character and nature of God, his relationship with his Son, Jesus Christ, and with the dynamic Holy Spirit. This book takes readers on a ride of wonder and wisdom. The illustrations will draw you in, the 'fun facts' will blow your mind, and the practical applications will solidify your faith. *Flash Theology* is an unprecedented feast in the Christian publishing world. You will read it and be filled to overflowing with the knowledge of the glory of the Lord."

Carol McLeod, Bible teacher, bestselling author, speaker, podcaster, blogger

"We all owe Jenny Randle and Brayden Brookshier a debt of gratitude for this wonderfully creative resource. They have successfully married the visual with the conceptual in a way that makes theology more concrete and enjoyable. Best of all, the single thread that shows through on every page is that all of theology is the discovery of God's love and kindness toward his creation. For both the seeker and the seasoned wishing to gain a better grasp on theology, I cannot recommend this book highly enough!"

Abdu Murray, speaker and author at Embrace the Truth

"Turning the pages of *Flash Theology*, I kept saying to myself, 'Wow. This book is just so cool.' It's a graphic show-and-tell of the gospel, an approachable explanation of who God is, and an invitation to get to know him much more intimately than you do now—all wrapped into one. The book connects the truths of the Bible with your everyday life in a fresh, helpful way."

Jennifer Dukes Lee, author of *Growing Slow* and *It's All Under Control*

"*Flash Theology* masterfully connects readers to deep truths about God in a fun and engaging way. Every church should offer this book as a resource or small group study to help others learn more about God and love doing it!"

JoAnn Johnson, executive pastor at Newbreak Church and director of credentialed women at SoCal Network of the Assemblies of God

"Practical and a bit playful, *Flash Theology* somehow finds a way to be systematic without systematically reducing the wonder of God and his gospel—a difficult task to be sure. This is the type of narrative discipleship that helps people locate their place and purpose in the great Story. Well done, Jenny and Brayden."

Addison Bevere, COO of Messenger International, author of *Words with God*

Jenny Randle and Brayden Brookshier

flash theology

A Visual Guide to Knowing and Enjoying God More

Jenny Randle and
Brayden Brookshier

flash theology

A Visual Guide to
Knowing and Enjoying
God More

DAVID C COOK™

transforming lives together

FLASH THEOLOGY
Published by David C Cook
4050 Lee Vance Drive
Colorado Springs, CO 80918 U.S.A.

Integrity Music Limited, a Division of David C Cook
Brighton, East Sussex BN1 2RE, England

The graphic circle C logo is a registered trademark of David C Cook.

The website addresses recommended throughout this book are offered as a resource
to you. These websites are not intended in any way to be or imply an endorsement
on the part of David C Cook, nor do we vouch for their content.

Details in some stories have been changed to protect the identities of the persons involved.

Unless otherwise noted, all Scripture quotations are taken from the ESV® Bible (The Holy Bible, English
Standard Version®), copyright © 2001 by Crossway, a publishing ministry of Good News Publishers. Used by
permission. All rights reserved. Scripture quotations marked CSB are taken from the Christian Standard
Bible®, Copyright © 2017 by Holman Bible Publishers. Used by permission. Christian Standard Bible® and
CSB® are federally registered trademarks of Holman Bible Publishers; NIV are taken from the Holy Bible,
New International Version®, NIV®. Copyright © 1973, 2011 by Biblica, Inc.™ Used by permission of Zondervan.
All rights reserved worldwide. www.zondervan.com. The "NIV" and "New International Version" are
trademarks registered in the United States Patent and Trademark Office by Biblica, Inc.™; NKJV are taken
from the New King James Version®. Copyright © 1982 by Thomas Nelson. Used by permission. All rights
reserved; NLT are taken from the Holy Bible, New Living Translation, copyright © 1996, 2015 by Tyndale
House Foundation. Used by permission of Tyndale House Publishers, Carol Stream, Illinois 60188. All
rights reserved. The authors have added italics and other effects to Scripture quotations for emphasis.

Library of Congress Control Number 2022935587
ISBN 978-0-8307-8474-5
eISBN 978-0-8307-8477-6

The Team: Michael Covington, Kevin Scott, James Hershberger, Jack Campbell, Susan Murdock
Cover Design and Interior Concept Design: Micah Kandros
Interior Design and Typesetting: Emily Weigel
Author Cover Bio Photos: Annalisa Joy Photography (Brayden); Ariana Brookshier (Jenny)

Printed in the United States of America
First Edition 2023

1 2 3 4 5 6 7 8 9 10

111622

Dear reader,

We dedicate this book to your local church.

In doing so, we celebrate your church's dedication to building
disciples and strengthening the faith of generations. We see you
as you learn to love like family, lead within your community,
contend for miracles, and serve in a way that brings God glory.

May the Church be unshakable with the truth of who God is.

Contents

For free resources geared toward personal devotion or group discussion, and for downloadable church materials, visit flashtheology.com.

A Note from Jenny & Brayden

A. W. Tozer famously wrote: "What comes into our minds when we think about God is the most important thing about us."[1] In other words, nothing is more important than knowing God—and nothing even comes close. But there's a problem. Many Christians think theology is only for scholars or the spiritually elite. But this simply isn't true. While theology is, in one sense, an academic discipline, it can also be understood as the art of knowing God. God invites us to know him, as we are fully known by him (see 1 Cor. 13:12).

We wrote *Flash Theology* for your joy and delight in God, so that you may abound in the truth and wonder of who he is! Who are we anyway? We are two friends who happen to be related (we both married into the Randle family). Brayden is an academic theologian and spiritual contemplative, and Jenny is a Bible teacher with a creative and relational bent in ministry. Check out our author bio for more information. We're both passionate for God to use these words to inspire action toward your relationship with him.

It is our conviction that *theology* is more than a fancy word for smart people to use. While it includes intellectual knowledge, it is far richer and more satisfying. Theology goes beyond the study of the character of God to the art of knowing the One who already knows you intimately and loves you still. Our prayer is that you connect with a personal God (**Father God**, **Lord Jesus**, and **Holy Spirit**) throughout the pages of this book. You may notice we find him to be *so* personal that we drop the "the" before Holy Spirit within our communication.

The more you know God personally, the more you can enjoy and appreciate him for who he is. That's why in this book we lead you through thirty-one bite-size truths, highlighting key aspects of who God is. Our hope is that these flashes of truth will bring to light any false beliefs or preconceived notions you may have about God and will strengthen your relationship with him!

Instead of feeling confused about theology or wondering if it even matters, it's time to gain greater confidence and wisdom and to foster deeper intimacy in your relationship with God. Theology matters because God matters. We hope you experience wonder and awe as you discover theological truths about the Trinitarian God of the Bible!

Jenny Randle & Brayden Brookshier

What Is Flash Theology?

Flash

Burst of bright light

Theos = God

The ology

The study of

Theology is important for everyone, but if it is too dense, it can be hard to digest. *Flash Theology* is our way of giving you crucial theological truths in readable, digestible chapters without compromising quality or depth. Each of the thirty-one readings makes a complicated truth about the character of God simple and understandable.

How to Use This Book

For free resources geared toward personal devotion or group discussion, including an 8-week small group guide and downloadable church materials, visit flashtheology.com. There are two key ways to use this book.

Personal Devotional

You can use this resource in your personal devotions to strengthen your faith, not only as a onetime read, but by referencing it again and again. Each chapter starts with an **In a Flash** statement that is foundational to our faith, and concludes with an **Apply This**, which is *just one example* of how to put these God-truths into action.

Group Discussion

You can discuss this book as a group using the free 8-week small group guide from the website. And since we believe this book is excellent for a book study, we have created additional downloadable resources to guide those who choose to facilitate group discussion around the content.

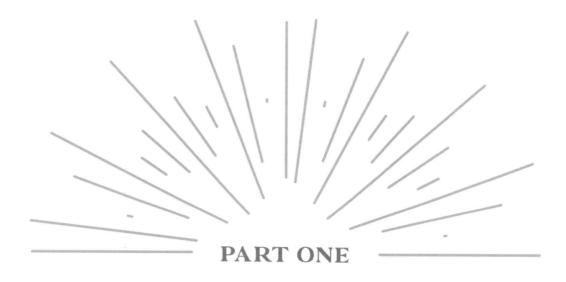

PART ONE

WHAT IS GOD?

When we ask what God is, we are inquiring about his triune nature. If this concept is new to you, stick with us! If you are already familiar with this concept, we hope to unpack God's nature in a fresh way. But first, it's important to establish that all theology is revelation and an invitation to be in an intimate relationship with God! This is where we will begin!

01

God Is the
Author of Life

IN A FLASH God is authoring the greatest love story ever told.

Hebrews 12:1-2 (NKJV)

Therefore we also, since we are surrounded by so great a cloud of witnesses, let us lay aside every

Ephesians 4:22

weight, and the sin which so easily ensnares us, and let us run with

1 Corinthians 9:24

endurance the race that is set before us, looking unto Jesus, the author and finisher of our faith, *who for the joy that was set before Him* **endured** *the cross, despising the shame, and has sat down at the right hand of the throne of God.*

Stories are connectors that cling straight to the soul. We believe God's story—shared in Scripture and overflowing into our own story—is the greatest love story ever told, as well as the most action-packed, suspense-filled, supernatural thriller ever written. And it's all true! To understand this story, you first need to know the author of the story.

Basic storytelling has three acts:

- **Act 1. Setup:** Establish the location and the characters.
- **Act 2. Confrontation:** Encounter plot twists and problems because of opposition and conflict.
- **Act 3. Resolution:** Resolve problems and bring closure.

God's love story uses the same structure:

- **Act 1. Beginning:** The stage is set with the pure design of creation and humanity.
- **Act 2. Broken:** The original design is tainted by disobedience to God, and the world falls into sin.
- **Act 3. Beautiful:** Brokenness is addressed and resolved through the death and resurrection of Jesus. The fullness of this redemption is found when Jesus returns and brings about the new creation.

The Whole Story of the Bible Points to Jesus

The triune God (**Father**, **Son**, **Holy Spirit**) is the main character and author of the greatest love story ever told. The story of Scripture contains this chain of events: creation, fall, redemption, and new creation; the overarching theme of the story points to Jesus.

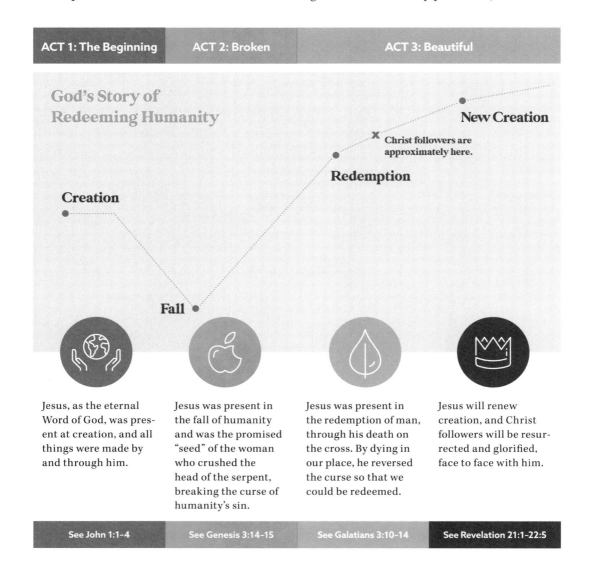

ACT 1: The Beginning	ACT 2: Broken	ACT 3: Beautiful	

God's Story of Redeeming Humanity

Creation

Fall

Redemption

x Christ followers are approximately here.

New Creation

Jesus, as the eternal Word of God, was present at creation, and all things were made by and through him.	Jesus was present in the fall of humanity and was the promised "seed" of the woman who crushed the head of the serpent, breaking the curse of humanity's sin.	Jesus was present in the redemption of man, through his death on the cross. By dying in our place, he reversed the curse so that we could be redeemed.	Jesus will renew creation, and Christ followers will be resurrected and glorified, face to face with him.
See John 1:1–4	See Genesis 3:14–15	See Galatians 3:10–14	See Revelation 21:1–22:5

WHAT HE IS

God reveals himself as the beginning and the end, the Alpha and Omega (Rev. 22:13). **As you read the Bible, it's imperative to realize that each story is part of one grand narrative. When you experience different chapters and journeys within your life, recognize that your life story** *also* **makes up one grand narrative.** To live your life abundantly well, you need to know the end of the story. Jesus is the hero of that story, and God is already restoring and will fully restore the broken things through him.

WHAT DOES THIS MEAN FOR ME?

Each day we live in the tension of a broken world that is already and not yet redeemed; we turn the page of a story written by God. The Old Testament demonstrated the need for a Savior and prophetically pointed to the Messiah. The New Testament showcases the life of the Messiah—the protagonist who conquered sin and death and sends Holy Spirit to build and strengthen the Church. Yet here we wait for the end of the story, in this place of living out and sharing the gospel in a broken world. In the waiting, Christ followers ache for the second coming of Christ. We endure plot twists and pain points as we turn each page of God's redeeming story. Yet even as the story unfolds, we know it is already complete. *And Jesus wins.*

May we not wander from the truth written in Scripture or be distracted from its mission of *reconciliation* through connection with God, who holds the power to fully redeem the brokenness of the world and connect his people with his beauty. Christ sustains and empowers us to persevere in our faith, even as his promises come to pass. Yet we endure in God's strength, not ours. God, not us, is the main character.

However, we are not born into a blank narrative. We are born into an evolving love story where we are the object of the author's love. He keeps writing our story, even through the trials and triumphs of life. Hardship and heartache strengthen us and invite us into deeper intimacy with him. We reflect on the moments of triumph because they reassure us, in times of crisis, that God is faithful, trustworthy, and good. God is inviting us toward himself daily as his story comes to resolution.

It is a beautiful thing to consider how our individual story relates to God's grand narrative. Our lives interweave and are interdependent. Each one has a divine purpose. When we understand our story in this way, we stand on holy ground and experience the sacred space God intended for us. As we actively participate in God's story, we have moments to demonstrate godly character and manifest his gifts to a world desperate for his transformative love. He invites us to be an instrument of promise and hope.

The narrative of creation, fall, redemption, and new creation parallels our individual need for the Savior. *We are designed to rely on him.* The weight of the world is too much for our shoulders, but not his. When our earthly story seems broken, under God's authorship, we can know that it is beautiful. **God will finish what he started, as he authors the greatest love story ever told.**

APPLY THIS: Set aside time today to meet Author God by practicing the spiritual discipline of praise and worship. Worship him in whatever circumstance you are experiencing in this season. Worship God simply because he is worthy and is authoring a redemptive story.

God Is Triune

02

IN A FLASH Triune God is one divine being in three distinct persons: **Father God, Lord Jesus, Holy Spirit.**

John 1:1 (NKJV)

Alluding to Genesis 1:1 ·······

Jesus ·······

In the beginning was the Word,

The Greek preposition infers face-to-face relationship ·······

Before everything was, Jesus was

and the Word was with God,

·····*Jesus*

Same word, different function

The Father

and the Word was God.

Jesus ·······

·······*Qualitative Term "God" or Deity*

WHAT HE IS

The Trinity is a tricky topic! Some use inadequate analogies, such as water or an egg, to describe the triune God. Neither of these describes the Trinity accurately, though. The following are two representations of the Trinity—a drawing and a table chart. Both visual aids show the same concept. We hope they help you understand the triune nature of God, since it is both edifying and foundational to our faith.

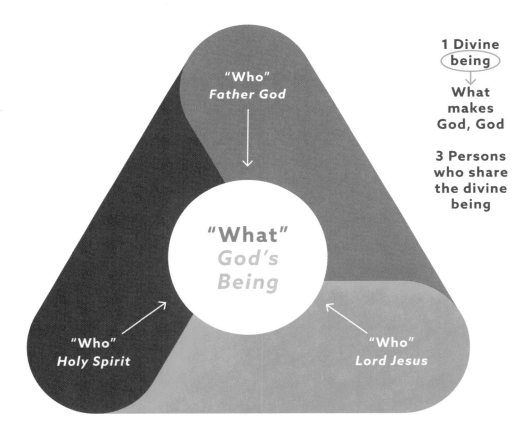

TRIUNE GOD

Triune God's "what" is *his one divine being* made up of multiple qualities.

Note: Jesus's "what" is God's divine nature and a human nature, due to his incarnation.

Triune God's "Who" is *three distinct persons* who equally share in the divine being.

- **"Who":** *Father God*
- **"Who":** *Lord Jesus*
- **"Who":** *Holy Spirit*

Father God is *not* Jesus. Jesus is *not* Holy Spirit. Holy Spirit is *not* the Father. The three "whos," however, *are* all one triune God, who are distinct in person.

There is one divine being called "God."

Let's time travel back to ancient Israel. For many centuries, Jewish people have made a practice of reciting the *shema*, found in Deuteronomy 6:4–5, which says: "Hear, O Israel: The LORD our God, the LORD is one. You shall love the LORD your God with all your heart and with all your soul and with all your might."

The *shema* is the heart of Jewish liturgy. The Hebrew word translated "one" in this passage is not the same word used for the number one. Instead, the word *'eḥād* speaks to God's unique being or essence. He is unique, unrivaled, and unparalleled. In other words, there is no one like our God! Ancient Israel was surrounded by nations who believed in many gods. At the time, the idea that God was **God alone** was counterintuitive. But Yahweh, the God of Israel, was determined to reveal himself as the one true God. *There is one God, and no one is like him!*

FUN FACT

The oneness of God is summarized in the word *monotheism*. While biblical authors do speak of other gods—perhaps referring to false gods or real spiritual powers of darkness—these so-called gods cannot rival the one true God in power or ability. They are not in any sense peers with Yahweh.

The being of God is shared by three distinct persons.

John 1:14 offers another astounding disclosure: "And the Word became flesh and dwelt among us, and we have seen his glory, glory as of the only Son from the Father, full of grace and truth."

The verse asserts that Jesus has existed throughout eternity with God the Father and became a human being at a specific point in time. Christian tradition refers to his becoming human as the *incarnation*. Jesus is God incarnate; he is Yahweh having become human. The miracle of the incarnation is that Jesus became everything we are (human) without ceasing to be everything he is (deity). He is the God-man. God personally entered his creation to rescue it! Part of his plan included sending his Spirit into the hearts of redeemed believers.

Many New Testament passages showcase the involvement of each distinct person of God in our Christian journey. Read the following passages to see some clear examples: Ephesians 4:4–6, Matthew 28:19, 2 Corinthians 13:14, and 1 Peter 1:2.

Each person of the Trinity is equally God.

These truths and more are the essence of what makes God, *God*, and each person of the Trinity (Father God, Lord Jesus, and Holy Spirit) equally possess and participate in the divine being. What makes God, God? Here are a few examples:

- **God is eternal.** He exists before all things and has no point of origin. He stands outside of space and time yet interacts with his creation. He is transcendent (above and beyond it all), yet he is immanent (present and pervasive in it all).

- **God is the Creator.** He created everything, both the visible and the invisible. The Creator is self-sufficient and self-sustaining, whereas his creatures are contingent. That is what his revealed name in the Hebrew Bible, Yahweh, means—the "I AM" is the self-sustaining One who has no beginning and no end. He *is*. He is I AM. As the Creator, he is the sovereign Lord over all creation. No one bosses him around. He is in charge!

- **God is infinite.** His essence, character, and attributes are not in progress and do not need improvement. If God were given an annual review of how he can improve his character, it would contain no suggestions, because he is perfect and without limitation. Whatever God is, he is limitless and flawless, even beyond what language can describe or define.

WHAT DOES THIS MEAN FOR ME?

Understanding the triune God in the proper way will grow your faith from generic to personable, as you fully encounter the different persons of the Trinity. And if nothing else, get this: you experience the Trinity even if you can't explain the Trinity. You interact with the persons of the triune God—consciously or subconsciously—even if you don't have articulate language to complement your experience.

Remember these three truths about the Trinity:

1. There is one divine being called God.
2. The being of God is shared by three distinct persons.
3. Each person of the Trinity is equally God.

APPLY THIS: Grab some colored markers (no-bleed markers work well for Bible pages). As you study your Bible, highlight the persons of the Trinity using the same color-coded technique you see throughout this book.

03

God Is
Relational

IN A FLASH The core of God's essence is relational because he is three in one.

John 14:20

In that day you will know that I am in my Father, and you in me, and I in you.

WHAT HE IS

The question came from a young child, maybe seven years of age. It was a good question, but it seemed impossible to answer, especially for a child. "What was God doing before he created everything? Was he bored?"

What *was* God doing before he created everything? We don't have any details, but we do know one thing: God was completely satisfied in a loving relationship even before he created anyone or anything else. So, no, God was not bored; he was enthralled by love. But where did this love come from? It came from himself—**Father, Son**, and **Holy Spirit**. He is a triune being, after all! No other world religion has anything like our triune God. No human imagination could have ever conceived it; God had to reveal it to us.

While every world religion claims that their god is loving, only the Christian God of Scripture can adequately match the claim of 1 John 4:8, "God is love." Why? Love is directional; it takes more than one person. It requires a lover and a beloved. Being love itself implies God has always had someone to love. Other so-called gods might have theoretically had the potential to love; but for them, love could not become a reality until they created someone to love.

The God of Scripture is unique. No analogy properly fits him, because every other being is unipersonal (one person who is one being), whereas God is tripersonal (one being who is three persons). Only the triune God can make the claim of being love to his very core, as an

 **FUN FACT**

Jesus is not God's Son in the same way that we are sons and daughters of God. Jesus is the Son of God in an entirely unique way. His sonship had no point of origin. He did not have a heavenly mother who conceived and delivered him. Jesus's relationship to God the Father is one where they equally share in the being of God, yet they relate to each other (analogously) as a father to a son in a way that is beyond our full comprehension.

eternal and essential attribute. Think about it this way: God is relational to the core because he is triune. There was never a time when God the Father did not have God the Son and Holy Spirit to love and be loved by, and vice versa.

When the Roman persecution of Christianity ended in AD 313, the Church was able to meet and flesh out key doctrines and dispel those that did not represent the teaching of Scripture. This theological work on the deity of Christ led to clearer ways of describing God's being. Words like *perichoresis* were used to help people understand the triune God. *Perichoresis* is a term that illustrates how the persons of the Trinity indwell one another. It's like three interlocking rings that are distinct yet together make up the whole.

This perichoretic relationship suggests two key things:

1. **The three persons of the Trinity experience mutual indwelling as they are fully and completely in one another.** It's like how Holy Spirit is both *with* us and *inside* us.

2. Each person of the Trinity is and has the full divine being (that which makes God, God). In other words, you cannot have Jesus without having the Father.

PERICHORESIS IN JOHN'S GOSPEL & LETTERS

EXAMPLE	VERSE	REFERENCE
The Father and Son's mutual indwelling assures that to interact with one is to interact with the other.	*"In that day you will know that I am in my Father, and you in me, and I in you."*	John 14:20
The Father and Son's mutual activity in Jesus's mission.	*"The Son can do … only what he sees the Father doing. For whatever the Father does, that the Son does likewise."*	John 5:19
The Father and Son's mutual message in Jesus's speech.	*"What I say, therefore, I say as the Father has told me."*	John 12:50
The Father and Son as mutually received by believers.	*"No one who denies the Son has the Father. Whoever confesses the Son has the Father also."*	1 John 2:23

While the Father, Son, and **Spirit** are distinct persons of the Godhead, they are inseparable in their perichoretic (mutual indwelling) relationship. Therefore, God is never—and has never been—without relationship, because he eternally experiences relationship within his triune being.

WHAT DOES THIS MEAN FOR ME?

Admittedly, this is a challenging concept to understand! It's because we are trying to use our finite brains and limited language to describe an infinite, unlimited God. God is relational, and his perichoretic relationship within himself reflects how he desires to relate to us.

The reason the triune God created everything, including you and me, is his desire to share and extend the joyous relationship he has within himself to glorified human beings (in the new creation). The triune God who indwells one another indwells us as a gift of grace. The original humans, Adam and Eve, were in relationship with God, but not quite the fullness of the perichoretic relationship we will one day have. We must be redeemed and glorified before we can experience the fullness of our relationship with God! Hints of this are present in Scripture passages where we are invited to share in fellowship with God's Son, or through the indwelling of Holy Spirit (1 Cor. 1:9; John 14:17; Rom. 8:9–11).

God also demonstrates his desire for relationship with us by including us in his mission to reconcile the world back to himself (2 Cor. 5:11–21). We are God's method to accomplish his mission, and we play a key role, even though God could accomplish all he wants without us. Why does he do it this way? Don't we hinder him with all our mess-ups and mistakes? **Since God is relational, he values relationships over efficiency. In fact, he values community, companionship, and collaboration with us even at the expense of efficiency!** A relationship with him is truly the most life-changing one we can ever have.

APPLY THIS: In your own words, summarize what you just learned in three to five sentences. How can we help people see that we are invited to be in relationship with a relational God?

04

God Is Savior

IN A FLASH Throughout Scripture, the triune God enacts a plan of salvation as the Savior of the world.

Isaiah 45:21-22

Declare and present your case;

let them take counsel together!

Who told this long ago?

Only God can command the events of history to work toward his intended goal

Who declared it of old? Was it

not **I,** the LORD? And there is

no other god besides me,

No spiritual power can rival God

a righteous God and a **Savior;**

Hosea 13:4

there is *none* besides me.

Turn │ to me │ and │ be saved,
·········· *Hebrew verb conveys to redirect the direction of the face*

all the ends of the earth! For I am

God, and there is no other.

WHAT HE IS

The Bible reveals the plot and promise of God to save the world. In reading Scripture, we learn about who God is and what he is like, all encapsulated in a *story*, which we discussed in chapter 1. The story tells God's plan of salvation.

The Old Testament reveals the twin pillars of Yahweh's identity as Creator and Redeemer (or "Savior"). Not only does this show us God's heart and deep commitment to his creation (even after the fall), it also sets the stage for God's climactic action of salvation as described in the New Testament.

What do we mean by salvation anyway?

THE GREEK VERB SŌZŌ,
"TO SAVE," APPEARS OVER

390

TIMES IN THE BIBLE

THE VERB SŌZŌ APPEARS

286

TIMES IN THE OLD TESTAMENT (LXX)

THE VERB
SŌZŌ APPEARS

106

TIMES IN THE
NEW TESTAMENT

80
OF THOSE TIMES
INVOLVE A KING GOING
TO WAR ON BEHALF
OF HIS PEOPLE

IT APPEARS
APPROXIMATELY

90

TIMES IN THE
PROPHETS

A complementary tension exists between the spiritual and sociopolitical connotations of the Messiah's saving activity (*sōzō*), which is best understood through the metaphor of exile. Rather than saving his original followers from the oppression of Rome, the Messiah's war had a greater aim: a new exodus from humanity's exile due to sin. The Greek text of Matthew 1:21 gives a clue to this, as it may be translated: "Since he [Jesus] will save his people *away from* their sins." The preposition *apo* portrays the saving activity as separation "away from" sins. The statement seems to personify sin as an enemy who had captured God's people and kept them hostage until the Messiah rescued them. This take on salvation supports the Bible's focus on a new exodus, with God's people being rescued not from an earthly empire but from the tyranny of sin and death into a fresh life with God.

It might be said that the Father *appointed* the plan of salvation, the Son *accomplished* salvation, and the Spirit *applies* the benefits of salvation to us. But the reality is a bit more complicated. Each person of the Trinity has a robust, layered role in salvation. While this can be seen throughout the New Testament, Paul's letter to the

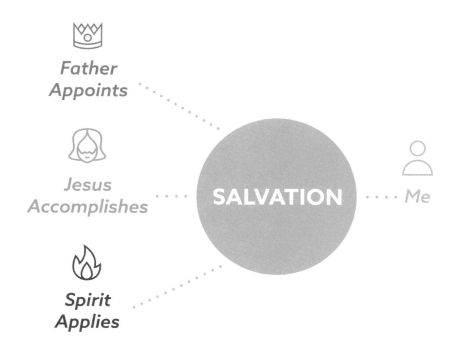

Father
Appoints

Jesus
Accomplishes

SALVATION

Me

Spirit
Applies

Ephesians is particularly brilliant in highlighting the unique roles of each member of the Trinity. Paul didn't explain the Trinity there so much as he described how the Trinity can be experienced, especially in terms of salvation.

WHAT DOES THIS MEAN FOR ME?

As you continue reading, you will see many unique facets of God's saving role and his heart that fuels his redemptive activity. Setting the foundation means seeing what we are saved *from* and what we are saved *for*. Because of the fall and sin, God has a plan of judgment to confront the root issue of his good world having gone wrong. This judgment is ultimately a good thing, but it also suggests there is genuine displeasure and grievance toward humanity's rebellion. This is often referred to as God's "wrath," which is one way of describing what Christians are saved from by having their sins forgiven and atoned for (1 Thess. 1:9–10; Rom. 5:9). So we are saved from God's judgment and for a renewed relationship with God, which includes new privileges and responsibilities "for good works," as Ephesians 2:10 says.

APPLY THIS: Read Ephesians 1 and identify each person of the Trinity's role in accomplishing or applying salvation.

05

God
Is Dwelling

IN A FLASH God is determined to dwell with his people in an unveiled manner.

Ephesians 2:19-22

So then you are no longer <u>strangers and aliens</u>, but you are

·············· — Hebrews 11:13

<u>fellow citizens</u> with the saints

Philippians 3:20, citizen of heaven ··········

and members of the household of

God, built on the foundation of the

apostles and prophets, Christ Jesus

himself being the | cornerstone,

··········· foundation

in whom the whole structure,

being joined together, grows into a

holy temple in the Lord. In *him*

1 Corinthians 3:16

you also are being built together

into a dwelling place for God

place to live

by the Spirit.

THE PLACE GOD'S PRESENCE DWELLS

See Revelation 21:3	New Creation*	God dwells face to face with his resurrected people in the new heavens and earth where God's manifest presence pervades all of creation.
See 1 Corinthians 3:16	God's People	God indwells his redeemed people by providing **Holy Spirit** as the temple presence of God, expanding his presence wherever they go.
See John 1:14	Jesus	God dwelt in human form through the Word becoming flesh. The incarnation of Jesus provided a pocket of heaven on earth everywhere he went.
See Exodus 25:8	Tabernacle	God dwelt with his priests in a confined physical location with the purpose of restoring his presence on earth. Priests met with God in the tabernacle and mediated his presence to the people.
See Genesis 1–2	Original Creation	God dwelt with his people in the Garden of Eden, and they bore his image. They were trusted to partner with God to bring the earth to its full intent.

*See connecting chart on page 27.

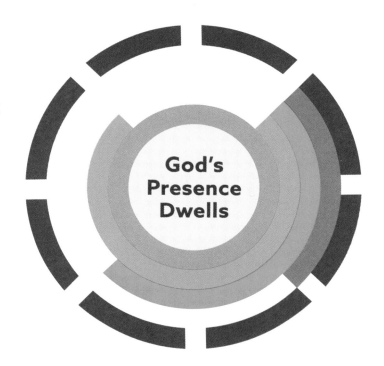

Humans' Closeness to God's Manifest Presence

New Creation
God's People
Jesus
Tabernacle
Original Creation

WHAT HE IS

The mission of God is woven throughout the Bible and is the foundation of its many covenant agreements. Jeremiah 31:33 says, "I will be their God, and they shall be my people" (see also Hos. 2:23; 2 Cor. 6:16; Heb. 8:10; Rev. 21:7). The mission of God is pervasive in the Bible! Covenants require both parties to carry out specific responsibilities to honor the promise and maintain the relationship. While humanity has a history of broken promises, God is a promise keeper who provides forgiveness and freedom as he restores our broken relationship.

God designed humanity for his enjoyment and ours, inviting us to be with him and reflect his likeness. Adam and Eve enjoyed God's presence in the Garden of Eden until they broke their covenant with him by eating forbidden fruit. A test of love became a betrayal instead, as our first parents told God, "We don't trust you." As a result, they could no longer experience a pure relationship with God; it became strained. Shame and sin cause mistrust, which fosters brokenness between God and his people.

God had a plan to dwell with humanity—a plan that began in Eden and reaches its apex in the future new creation (Rev. 21:1–22:5). God didn't just snap his fingers. He followed a process, wooing us and winning us over to his love. Flash forward from Eden, and God created a dwelling place where he could be experienced at one physical location: the tabernacle (which later became the temple). In Exodus 25:8, the Lord said to Moses, "Let them make me a sanctuary, that I may dwell in their midst." (Highlight, circle, or underline that word "dwell"; it's our keyword!) This sanctuary was the ark of the covenant kept first in the tabernacle, then in the temple in Jerusalem. It was a marker for the portable dwelling place where God's sacred presence would rest, a place where priests and religious leaders would bring animal sacrifices to atone for the sins of God's people. While it was God's design, the sacrificial system was temporary; it was intended not as a permanent fix but as a signpost. The covenant was based on conditional promises—if Israel was obedient to God, he would bless them. If they disobeyed, there would be consequences.

Dun, dun, dun. In 1 Samuel 4, the Israelites turned the purity of God's sacrificial system into poison. As they warred with the Philistines, they began to treat the ark of the covenant as a magical object to protect them against evil, danger, and disease, and bring them victory in battle. When in danger, instead of calling on God, they called for the ark. They wanted God's protection but not his company. It was classic genie-in-a-bottle theology. They worshipped the container instead of its Creator. The Old Testament is filled with stories of

FUN FACT

When John 1:14 says that Jesus "dwelt" among us, the Greek verb is from *skēnoō*, which is used in the Old Testament as the verb for God's "tabernacling" presence. It's more than an ordinary way of dwelling; it is the residence of sacred space—God with us!

God's people missing the mark on what God was ultimately trying to do. They needed a Savior. And they knew it.

Now we flash forward to the first century and the Gospels, where we learn that Christ did not come to destroy the law, but to fulfill it (Matt. 5:17). John 1:14 says, "The Word became flesh and dwelt among us, and we have seen his glory, glory as of the only Son from the Father, full of grace and truth." This passage refers to the incarnation of Jesus, in which God became human. With God arriving in human form, there was no longer a need for a physical tabernacle or temple to represent God's dwelling place. Jesus became the temple, a tabernacle formed as a physical person—divine, powerful, perfect, and ministering to the world around him.

Jesus is the solution to our separation from God. He gave his life to give us abundant life, and that abundant life means a life in community with the triune God. That's where the Jesus story takes us. It doesn't end with Jesus rising from the dead and ascending to heaven, and our hope being "out of this world." God's mission, as Ephesians 1:10

IN THE NEW CREATION, THE MANIFEST PRESENCE OF THE TRIUNE GOD WILL BE:

Perfect *unveiled in quality*	Something that is perfect is the absolute ideal; flawless; it has no room for improvement.
Pervasive *comprehensive in scope*	Every speck of creation will be flooded with God's life, love, and presence. It will cover every square inch of the resurrected cosmos.
Permanent *everlasting in duration*	Something that is permanent has no end; it does not fade; it will endure forever and ever.

reminds us, is to unite all things, in heaven and earth, into a beautiful marriage of the two worlds (we call this *new creation*). Just as God's "tabernacling" presence shows up in the Old Testament and the incarnation of Jesus, it also shows up in Revelation 21:3 (see the graphic earlier in this chapter), where the story of God's dwelling presence reaches its intended aim. God will one day delight in our company as we, all the redeemed, will delight in his presence.

Have you ever considered enjoying God as the highest aim of human existence? The Westminster Catechism speaks of the highest aim of humanity in this way: "Man's chief end is to glorify God and enjoy him forever." This implies a constant communion between the human and the divine presence. The end goal of God's plan includes having his presence with us in a way that is perfect (unveiled in quality), pervasive (comprehensive in scope), and permanent (everlasting in duration). This is worth repeating. We call this the "3 Ps."[2]

Although God is now "with us," his unhindered manifest existence is not here in its entirety yet. But it will be. For the first time, God will fully and forever make his home on earth where all creation will experience his presence like never before. **Heaven and earth will be joined together, void of sin, sorrow, and suffering. It will be a wedding between the two worlds, where God's dwelling space and ours unite, one and the same, for eternity.**

WHAT DOES THIS MEAN FOR ME?

Through a relationship with Jesus, **Holy Spirit** dwells within us. Because of this, we live fulfilled, fruitful lives, on mission, reconciling people to God. Our body is a temple where God resides. Our life becomes a tabernacle for the presence of God (see, for example, Rom. 8:9–11).

One day, we'll be in perfect fellowship with the triune God, without sin or temptation. When the kingdom of God comes in its fullness (*new creation*), God's presence will be manifest with us. Eternity awaits us, but as we wait, we have the very presence of God here and now, leading us, comforting us, inviting us to worship him! He isn't confined, but free. He isn't far, but near. When the brokenness or pain of the world gets to us, we know who dwells within. Remember, we get to respond to the gift-giving guest who resides in the home of hearts. As we dwell close to him in the waiting, he mobilizes his people in power and purpose to provide beauty to a broken world.

APPLY THIS: It is a privilege to commune with God. Spend twenty minutes in silence with God, reflecting on the fact that you are with him. If he says anything to you, write it down. If he gives you an experience of his peace or joy or another fruit of the Spirit, journal about it.

06

God Is Inherently Holy

IN A FLASH God's holiness is out of this world yet held within it.

1 Peter 1:16

cited from Leviticus 11:44

Since it is written,

"You shall be holy, for I am holy."

set apart

WHAT HE IS

What comes to mind when you think of the word *holy*? Some connect holiness to perfection, power, or reverence—all of which are true. **Holiness is moral by association but transcendent by nature.** *Slow down and read that sentence again.* Holiness is both out of this world yet held within it. In other words, holiness is what designates common things or people as sacred. It gives extraordinary meaning to the otherwise ordinary.

SCRIPTURE SHARES TWO FACETS OF GOD'S HOLINESS:

From Creation ······· *God is set apart* ······· *with his people*

GOD IS SET APART FROM CREATION

God is holy; therefore, he exists completely apart from his creation (Ps. 96:9). He's spotless, perfect, and powerful. God's nature is completely unique and unmistakable, and nothing about him is defiled by sin (Rev. 15:4). God's name, fame, and personality are "holy and awesome" (Ps. 111:9). There is no one like him, nor will there ever be (Ex. 15:11).

GOD IS SET APART WITH HIS PEOPLE

"You shall be holy to me, for I the LORD am holy and have separated you from the peoples, that you should be mine" (Lev. 20:26). God is set apart, yet he displays his holiness by being near to his children. He is holy and high and lifted up yet decides to dwell with us (Isa. 57:15). Because of our relationship with Christ, we too stand on holy, sacred ground, bowing with reverence, wonder, and awe at our Creator. Our status changed from sinner to saint—from unholy to holy. First Peter 2:9 even refers to the community of redeemed believers as a "holy nation."

In thinking about God's holiness and how he relates to us, it is helpful to consider his holiness like a fire. Hebrews 12:29 says that "God is a consuming fire" (cited from Deuteronomy 4:24). "Consuming" here in the original Greek means "to destroy completely."[3]

The fire of Pentecost didn't stop in Acts 2; it set things in motion. As Holy Spirit indwells, he sparks a passion inside of us for more of himself. Not only does God's holiness refine and purify, it destroys too. Raging like a wildfire, God burns up dry and dead things, clearing the ground for new life to begin. Jesus scorches sin and sets us ablaze to develop godly fruit, make disciples, and live faithfully for him. As we stoke the fire of God within our lives, he ministers through us, sparking a revival to set the captives free and change the landscape of the whole community.

In Israel's temple, the priests had access to the presence of God. To make them morally and ceremonially pure—ready to enter his presence—God gave them laws, rules, and rituals (see Leviticus, for example). These rituals were intended to teach God's people about his holiness. But they were not intended to be permanent institutions; they were signposts, leading the story of Scripture toward Jesus, the ultimate cleansing sacrifice (Heb. 10:10–14). God makes us holy in Christ. Period. Nothing we do can earn that status marker before God.

WHAT DOES THIS MEAN FOR ME?

Have you ever seen gold melted down? When exposed to fire, gold shines brighter. Pure gold is indestructible as it sits within the dangerously hot flames. Fool's gold, or pyrite, looks like the real thing until it is exposed to the fire. As it sits in the flames, it darkens, begins to smell like rotten eggs, and eventually becomes brittle and broken. Fire can reveal one's true colors and character.

The holy fire of God can reveal someone's true colors and character, as well as bring them back to life. Holiness is not a behavior leading to an achievement; it's the crux of a Christian's identity, imparted and received by grace. We are set apart, and as we act as ones set apart, our identity takes shape. (In fact, it is because we are declared to be holy that we can have a relationship with a holy God.) Through our relationship with Jesus, we don't need to perform religious acts to get close to God. Jesus lived a sinless, holy, and blameless life that paved the path for us. In Christ, we are purified (1 John 3:3), and we grow into the precious sons and daughters we were created to be. Meanwhile, some are impure fool's gold and will reap the consequences of their actions within God's purifying fire.

We are holy because God molded us with purpose and passion. God is holy in that he is the purpose and drives our passion. Our holiness is about being set apart rather than behaving a certain way. The action of holiness is just the by-product of our identity as saints. When we are saved, sin no longer controls us. We are saints who receive comfort, love, and guidance from our Savior. He sends spiritual fire to destroy our sin and purify us (Ps. 51:10). As the purifying fire burns, we begin to live the holiness we've already been given (sanctification).

Have you ever seen or studied the purification process of gold? Twenty-four-karat gold is pure, without any trace of other metals. Here is how fire can be used to purify gold:

FUN FACT

The English word *saints* comes from the plural form of the Greek adjective *hagios*. It literally means "holy ones" and often refers to believers (see examples in Ephesians 1:1 and 2 Corinthians 1:1).[4]

1. Gold scraps are placed in a crucible, a container that can withstand high heat, and then the crucible is placed in a fire.

2. The fire is stoked, hotter and hotter, until it reaches gold's melting point (1,948°F).

3. The fire reshapes the gold, and any impurities or other metals rise to the top.

4. The crucible is removed from the fire and the other metals and impurities are removed.

This is similar to the process of sanctification in our lives. As Christ followers, we are God's precious children. Our crucible (life) experiences a process of refining (sanctification). When we spend time with God, through practicing spiritual disciplines, the fire is stoked. As the prince of preachers, Charles Spurgeon, once said, "Let us use texts of Scripture as fuel for our heart's fire, they are live coals; let us attend sermons, but above all, let us be much alone with Jesus."[5] And while we abide with Jesus, God removes the impurities and imperfections, and we are molded by God toward the image of Jesus (Rom. 8:29).

APPLY THIS: Review the spiritual disciplines above. These are a few ways in which we live according to our holy identity. Intentionally practice fellowship by making time to attend a local Bible-teaching church and fellowship with other believers.

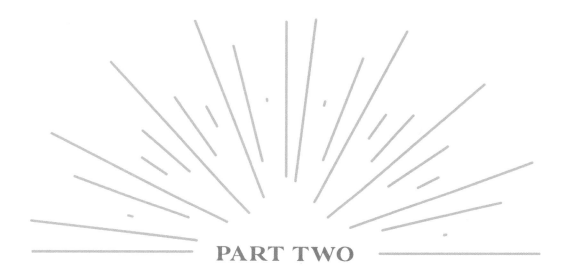

PART TWO

WHO IS GOD?

The next part of our journey explores the identity of God through his relational roles. It may help to think of this section as a mosaic, with many individual portraits that come together to provide one robust image. Sound theology encourages seeing each portrait, but always within the grand picture of the mosaic. Building on the foundation we have established—namely, that the triune God has been authoring a story in which he seeks to redeem us so that he can dwell with us in a holy relationship—we turn our attention to the ways in which our awesome God chooses to relate to us. These relational roles are uniquely distinct yet make up the grand picture of who God is and how each person of the Trinity participates in relationship to us. Understanding these relational roles gives your life its true meaning, now and into eternity.

07

God Is Our King

IN A FLASH God is the King who entered his creation to conquer hearts and win the world back to his loving reign.

Revelation 19:11-13, 16

Then I saw heaven opened, and

King Jesus returns to earth

behold, a white horse! The one sitting

on it is called Faithful and True,

See Revelation 3:14

and in righteousness he judges and

makes war. His eyes are like a flame

The last war to end

of fire, and on his head are many

These descriptions are meant to heighten our awe at his glory and power

diadems, and he has a name written

that no one knows but himself. He is clothed in a robe dipped in blood, and the name by which he is called is The Word of God.... On his robe and on his thigh he has a name written, King of kings and Lord of lords.

Jesus is the highest and greatest of all kings

The symbol-laden, vivid language of Revelation 19 gives us an apt and awe-inspiring view of our Lord, who is indeed the "King of kings" (19:16). Reading this description, it is easy to forget how humble the King was in how he entered the world on that first Christmas. Let's start by reminiscing on the underappreciated storyline of Advent and how it contributes to the theme of God as King.

WHO HE IS

Many of us read Matthew 2 every Christmas season—and rightfully so! We enjoy getting into the Christmas spirit, with the festivity, food, and fun, but we also like rehearsing the drama that occurred that first Christmas. It was much crazier than any family drama we might have with relatives during the holidays!

The story of Christmas is about a clash of kings and kingdoms. It is a conflict of crowns between the kings of the world and the true King who has come into the world. King Herod was a malicious, violent, and brutal man. His paranoia of someone taking his throne led him to kill many people, including his own sons. It is not surprising, then, that Herod didn't receive the news of Christ's birth politely. He perceived it as a direct challenge to his kingship.

 **FUN FACT**

In his gospel, Matthew proclaimed Jesus as King and, from the beginning (1:1; 2:2), set out to show that Jesus was heir to David's throne. He took a great interest in David, mentioning him five times in 1:1–17 (seventeen times total in Matthew). The title "Son of David" was applied to Jesus seven times in the book (1:1; 9:27; 12:23; 15:22; 20:30–31; 21:9, 15), which was part of Matthew's many intentional uses of the number seven.

Matthew emphasized that Jesus is more than a baby boy who happened to be born in Bethlehem. He is the "Son of David" (1:1) and "Immanuel" (1:23). "Son of David" is a statement of royal identity that carries with it the responsibility of rescuing God's people and bringing forth the kingdom of God through righteousness and peace. Matthew often deployed the title when Jesus was called to rescue people from an ill or oppressive condition. This was no coincidence or misstep. The Son of David was the promised one who would bring about eschatological (*end-time* or *end-goal*) deliverance from the oppression of darkness, and healing as a foretaste of the ultimate restoration. In this regard, Jesus truly is Immanuel, the tangible presence of God with people—the One who rescues people from their sins and the consequences of such sins (1:21).

After learning that the Messiah was to be born in Bethlehem (Matt. 2:6, citing Mic. 5:2), the magi made their way to Jerusalem, following the transient star. Magi were "men of wisdom who studied the stars."[6] They were concerned with what the movement of the stars (as signs or omens) might signify for the future affairs of history, like the birth of a king. **The magi's astrological knowledge and appreciation did not lead them to worship the stars but allowed the stars to point them to the true King who they should worship—Jesus.** It is a noteworthy example of a notably pagan practice being utilized in a commendable way.

The magi came with the goal to worship Christ (Matt. 2:2, 11). Matthew 2:11 tells us that when the magi entered the house where the infant Jesus was, "they bowed down and worshiped him" (NIV). Although some view this worship as merely the act of prostrating oneself in the presence of a king, Matthew's verb implies more; he used it to describe true worship.[7] It is perhaps surprising that the first people (according to Matthew) to regard Christ as King were the magi—who were pagan Gentiles. The birth narrative of Christ enlightens us on one of Matthew's primary themes of the Messiah's identity: his royal kingship. Not only is he "King of the Jews" but King of the whole world. The magi foreshadowed the "many" who were later to come from east and west to take their place in the kingdom of heaven (Matt. 8:11; see also Rev. 15:3–4). The appearance of magi from the East (pagan land) to worship Jesus was a jaw-dropping display of Christ's intention to become King of the whole world.

Christmas is the reminder that the King of Heaven is also the King of Earth. The newborn King came to win back what was lost at the fall. He is the King who comes to save and unite heaven and earth under his kingship! He will reign forevermore and has already begun to take back his world.

WHAT DOES THIS MEAN FOR ME?

When Isaac Watts wrote the famous ballad "Joy to the World," he didn't intend to limit its use to the Advent season. While the hymn speaks of the first coming of Jesus, Watts primarily wrote it in anticipation of Christ's second coming, utilizing Psalm 98 as a prophetic Old Testament passage about Christ the King's glad return to establish his eternal kingdom.[8] Thus, the famous line in the song: "Let earth receive her king!" And so all the lyrics serve to elevate our spirits and bolster our theology of God's rule and reign, both now and in the world to come when he returns, resulting in the ends of the earth seeing "the salvation of our God" (Ps. 98:3).

Receiving the kingdom of heaven means receiving God as your King and the benefits that come from enjoying his reign and rule. The Old Testament establishes that God rules over all; thus, the kingdom of heaven should not be understood as a retreat from the world, but as the kingdom that will inevitably pervade the world.

No king, queen, or government can ever be what it is supposed to be until God becomes King, which is a major part of the salvation plan. That's because everything is designed by God and thrives best when under his sovereign care. This means people—like you and me—have to receive him as King. The moment we trust Jesus, we are giving him our allegiance and loyalty. At that moment, he is enthroned not only in heaven but also in our hearts. One day, the whole world will see the glory of the King of Kings, and we will enjoy his rule in the world to come. Will you let this King ascend the throne of your heart?

THE THREE PARTS OF A KINGDOM IN CHRISTIAN THEOLOGY

Yahweh, the triune God, is the King (Ps. 47:2).

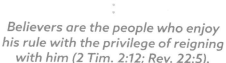

*Believers are the people who enjoy
his rule with the privilege of reigning
with him (2 Tim. 2:12; Rev. 22:5).*

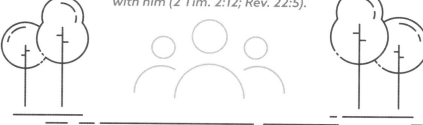

*The future resurrected cosmos, constituting the
"new heaven and new earth" (see Rev. 21:1–22:5), is the
destined place of the kingdom's eternal residence.*

APPLY THIS: Think about God being King over your heart
and life. Journal about the areas in which his reign has yet
to take effect. How can you begin to surrender those areas
to God as your King?

08

God Is Our Father

⚡ **IN A FLASH** God is my true heavenly father who loves me incomparably and unconditionally.

Romans 8:14-17

For all who are led by the Spirit of God are sons of God. For you did not receive the spirit of slavery to fall back into fear, but you have received the Spirit of adoption as sons, by whom we cry, "Abba! Father!"

An endearing way of referring to a dad ⋯⋯⋯⋯

The Spirit himself bears witness

⋯⋯⋯⋯ *Like a lawyer advocating on our behalf*

with our spirit that we are _children_

of God, and if children, then heirs—

heirs of God and fellow **heirs with**

Everything Christ will possess in the kingdom, we will share.

Christ, _provided we suffer_

with him _in order that we may_

also be glorified _with him._

WHO HE IS

Documenting three years of ministry, the Gospels provide a lens into the key themes Jesus emphasized in his teaching. One key theme was learning to embrace God as Father.

Jesus's prayer for his followers includes a majestic revelation of his heart for you and me. He prayed to his Father that the Church would be united "so that the world may know that you sent me and loved them <u>even as</u> you loved me" (John 17:23). Some people are drawn to the gospel to experience the Father's love for them—the same love he bestowed on Jesus in eternity past. The Greek conjunction *kathōs*, translated "even as," is packed with power. Even as the Father loves Jesus, he loves *you*. **God the Father spoils us with the same quality of love he gives his divine Son.** Mind blown? Ours too! Marinate on that for a while. And when you need a reminder, read John 17:26, where Jesus prayed for the Father's love to be in his followers as it is in him.

Think about it this way: Part of being a disciple of Jesus is learning to posture ourselves under the endless love of the Father. Like a basin beneath a waterfall, we are to live under the powerful and unceasing adoration of the eternal Father.

Paul also celebrated this relational role of God. He wanted us to understand that being a child of God is not something we are by default but a gift that comes with the new life in Christ. Romans 8:14–17 is one of the most important of Paul's writings on the subject. Interestingly, Paul used the metaphor of adoption here. In Paul's Greco-Roman context, adoption had major ramifications. The adopted child's debts and legal obligations were paid in full, they received the name and inheritance

FUN FACT

The Bible is peppered with passages that ascribe maternal attributes to God. For example, Isaiah 49:15 compares God to a compassionate, nursing mother. Isaiah 66:13 likens God to a mother who comforts and nurtures her child. The point is that he is the ultimate, perfect parent—embodying both masculine traits and feminine traits.

of their new father, and they attained equal status to their adopted dad. The child became a legitimate member of the family. In Paul's day, in the Greco-Roman world, adoption was a dignifying practice that elevated the life of the adopted child, regardless of their age.

Spiritual adoption means the Father adopts us as his very own, giving us benefits far beyond even those in the Greco-Roman world. He forgives our debt of sin, which corresponds with the Lord's Prayer, in how we call God Father and are taught to pray for him to forgive our debts (Matt. 6:9, 12). The Father gives us an eternal inheritance, culminating in a resurrected body and a co-reign with him over a resurrected universe (Rom. 8:17–25). It's like the scene from *The Lion King* when Mufasa says to his son: "Simba, everything the light touches is our kingdom." In the new creation, every inch of creation will be touched by divine light, and the Father will say something similar to us as he invites us to take his hand to rule with him for eternity. And we are, even now, members of his family (Rom. 8:16; Eph. 2:19) as we await the full privileges of being God's children.

However, adoption has its limitations as a metaphor. God is our Creator and desires to be in a fond relationship with us as our Father. Because of sin, we separated and alienated ourselves from God. So the Father orchestrated a plan—moving heaven and earth to bring us home to his family. That's where the adoption metaphor comes in. We now belong to the Father as his legitimate sons and daughters. But this is more than a change of legal status; God transforms our spiritual DNA as we surrender more of our heart to him.

Holy Spirit works as our advocate here, acting as our lawyer and testifying that we are indeed sons and daughters of the Father. That's the point of Romans 8:16: "The Spirit himself bears witness with our spirit that we are children of God." All of this, in the context of Romans 5–8, is about how the Father sees us as he sees Jesus, because we are "in Christ."

Our relationship with God is not a fickle one, where every time we sin, our security of salvation is undone. Minister John Stott said, "When we sin, we do not lose our relationship to him as children, though our fellowship with him is spoiled until we confess and turn away from our sin.... To put it another way, we can be justified only once; but we need to be forgiven every day."[9] **As a believer, sin will not dissolve the status of your relationship with God. However, sin will diminish the experience of your**

relationship with God. That's one of the reasons why sin is egregious; it robs us of experiencing and enjoying the benefits of a faithful relationship.

When there is any strain in our relationship with God, we know who is at fault *(cough, cough: you and me)*. But the Father does not disown us because of our current struggle against sin. He disciplines us with loving correction (Heb. 12:4–13), but he will never abandon us (Heb. 13:5).

How do we know God will never cease to love us? His love for us has always been and always will be. God's fatherly love toward us is unconditional. We can come to our heavenly dad with confidence that we are always going to be received—with arms wide open—as his beloved sons and daughters. And in his family, we are all his favorites; he is that good, because our true dad is the infinite God!

> For you did not receive the
> spirit of slavery to fall back into fear, but
> ## you have received the Spirit of adoption
> as sons, by whom we cry, "Abba! Father!"
>
> (ROM. 8:15)

WHAT DOES THIS MEAN FOR ME?

Do you ever have times when you are doing something ordinary, but then a God-moment happens and makes it one of your most extraordinary memories? I (Brayden) was taking my son, Kairo, for a walk when something unforgettable happened. My then-four-month-old baby boy loved to be outside and go for walks. I recall pushing him in his stroller along the bay on a warm San Diego evening, staring at him and thinking, *Kairo will never know how much I love him.* I meant it. I honestly don't know how he will ever comprehend it! *I will tell him those words all the time, but can the words even encapsulate how I feel about my son?*

That's when God, our heavenly dad, spoke to my heart (internally) with such clarity and fervor that I know it was him. It was like a gentle whisper, but with the tenacity of a raging river, he said, *"Now you finally know how I feel about you."* I didn't walk the rest of the way home; I floated. I was gripped by the love of the Father. For once in my life, I didn't push back or stifle God's love for me; I simply received it. It was nothing short of magical to simply breathe in that experiential truth. It was one of those experiences that will forever anchor my faith.

Human relationships provide only an imperfect metaphor of how we relate to God. First, many of us have a negative view of one or both of our parents. We must learn that God is not our parents or the mistakes they made. He is holy and perfect, and his love outweighs the love of even the best parents. If we're parents, one day our kids will grow up and move out, and while we hope to always be close with them, it won't be the day-to-day life it is when they are young children.

Uniquely though, human beings were not created to graduate to an existence of autonomy—to a life apart from God, where he has his life and we have ours, and our lives intersect only a few times per calendar year. On the contrary, life with God is where we find true flourishing in an ever-present, hand-in-hand relationship with our loving Father. Perhaps that is why Matthew tells about Jesus exhorting his listeners to "become like little children" (Matt. 18:3 NIV). Could it be that the best aspects of parenthood are a foretaste of how we will relate to God as Father in eternity? The Bible seems to speak of it as such. After all, you and I are destined for a perpetual, intimate, perfect relationship with God. May we embrace living like his children now and forevermore!

APPLY THIS: Pray specifically about God's fatherly love and that you'll notice and respond when he lovingly inspires, corrects, and equips you to be who he has created you to be.

09

God Is
Our Mediator

IN A FLASH Jesus is the one and only mediator between God and mankind.

1 Timothy 2:5-6 (NIV)

For there is one God and one **mediator** between God

·········· *a person who stands between two parties* ··········

and <u>mankind</u>, the man Christ Jesus,

who gave himself as a

ransom for all people. This has

see Matthew 20:28 ··········

now been witnessed to at

the proper time.

WHO HE IS

During the Christmas season, you may find it fulfilling to decorate the exterior of your house, at least until you try to fit that three-pronged plug for your new string of lights into an older two-slot outlet. Once powered up, those Christmas lights will shine down the block, but as much as you force the plug to connect right now, it just won't. The lights remain unlit, unable to reflect the goodness of the holidays like years prior.

Remembering traditions and experiences from the past will not change the fact that the cord cannot connect to the power in the present. It is lacking something. So your dad, who loves you so very much, sends you a go-between. He knows the only thing that will connect the three-pronged plug to the two-slot power outlet is an adapter. With the right adapter, the lights can be plugged in and connected to the source of the power. *Following what we're saying?* We were the unlit light bulbs until all-knowing Father God sent us Jesus—humanity's go-between.

Biblical theology shows that beginning with the fall, a mediator has been needed. People were separated from God by disobedience and sin. Romans 3:23 shares that we've all sinned and fall short of the glory of God. So how do we encounter God's presence despite our defiance?

In the Old Testament, God used mediators, like high priests, to define covenants that allowed people to connect to the presence of God. However, this connection was only temporary. The New Testament offers a permanent solution through the superior High Priest, Jesus (Heb. 4:14–16). He is the mediator that brings us into permanent connection with the Father by atoning for our sins and making amends with God through his death, resurrection, and ascension. **Jesus not only connects us to Father God through salvation but**

FUN FACT

Biblical theology studies a particular theme throughout all pages of Scripture. It takes careful interpretation as one explores the original context and overall grand narrative of the Bible.

also mediates our sanctification as we live set apart. As we endure in our Christian faith, Jesus mediates between the Father and us through intercessory prayer (Rom. 8:34; Heb. 7:22–28).

JESUS IS OUR MEDIATOR

In **Hebrews 8:6**, the author of Hebrews wrote to Jewish Christians, "But in fact the ministry Jesus has received is as superior to theirs as the covenant of which he is **mediator** is superior to the old one, since the new covenant is established on better promises" (NIV).

Hebrews 9:15 reads, "For this reason Christ is the **mediator** of a new covenant, that those who are called may receive the promised eternal inheritance—now that he has died as a ransom to set them free from the sins committed under the first covenant" (NIV).

Hebrews 12:22–24 says, "But you have come to Mount Zion, to the city of the living God, the heavenly Jerusalem. You have come to thousands upon thousands of angels in joyful assembly, to the church of the firstborn, whose names are written in heaven. You have come to God, the Judge of all, to the spirits of the righteous made perfect, to Jesus the **mediator** of a new covenant, and to the sprinkled blood that speaks a better word than the blood of Abel" (NIV).

WHAT DOES THIS MEAN FOR ME?

There is only one mediator. We cannot connect with God in a covenant relationship through religious tradition, a best friend's relationship with God, or acts of service. Jesus is our reconciler, bringing us into a relationship with Father God. Upon salvation, Christ gives us Holy Spirit, who is our counselor and advocate (see chapter 15).

We are set apart to shine in a dull world. But a war is being waged to break that connection and separate us from the very God who powers our lives. Satan sets out to steal, kill, and destroy our relationship (John 10:10). Because of our connection to God, Satan does not have authority over our story. Oh, he may try to seize control, but Jesus is contending for us. **Jesus is standing at the right hand of Father God petitioning on our behalf for the enemy to flee, because we've already been set free.**

Let's go back to our Christmas lights analogy. Sometimes the fuse gets blown, and the light goes out. How many times have you felt that way in your own life? As you plug into Christ, God powers you up to shine into a world desperate for meaning and purpose. Without him, the world is dark, dim, and devoid of light, love, and the true life God intends to give.

APPLY THIS: Study Hebrews 8:6. Write out the verse and read it a couple of times. Then slowly read the entirety of Hebrews 8. Answer these questions: What is the context in which verse 6 was written? What is the meaning of the text? Then prayerfully consider: How can I apply this to my life?

God Is Our Friend

 IN A FLASH God is a faithful friend who enjoys our company and helps us in times of need.

Revelation 3:20

Behold, **I** stand at the door and
Jesus

knock. If anyone hears *my* voice
Luke 12:36–37   *Anyone means ANYONE*

and opens the door, I will come

in to him and eat with him,
In the ancient world, to open your table to someone was to open your life to them.

and he with *me*.

WHO HE IS

"God is my friend? That sounds too casual or even irreverent. Isn't he holy and righteous and all those other things?" These are valid questions. The shocking thing about being friends with God is that friendship is a title for peers, typically reserved for those of equal status. But we are not peers or of equal standing with God! Regardless of status, God has chosen to relate to us, among other ways, as his friend.

Recall that Abraham was considered a friend of God (Isa. 41:8; James 2:23). Was Abraham's friendship with God a one-off or a paradigm of Judeo-Christian experience? According to church history, the latter seems to be the case. It is surprising how many people across history and the globe speak of God as our friend.

But this is not just contrived; Jesus developed a reputation of being a "friend of sinners" (Matt. 11:19; Luke 7:34; 15:2). How amazing that he didn't ask messy people to pretend to have it all together. **He never sinned and never condoned sin, but he practiced a transformational type of inclusion where he would befriend broken people and, *through his friendship*, make them whole.** We are glad to have friends that we can share the *real* with! It is exhausting to try to put on a show or wear a mask when you just want to share authentic life—the good, the bad, and everything in between—with friends.

Jesus even referred to his disciples as "friends" (John 15:15), indicating that they were insiders regarding God's grand plan. Isn't that what friends do? They share the inside scoop with one another. And like Abraham being a friend of God, the disciples being friends of Jesus is meant to apply to any future disciple too. You and I, as followers of Jesus, are his friends.

Take a few minutes and list out all the attributes and qualities that make for a good friend. Now, which of those does God lack? None! In fact, he has an infinite supply of every praiseworthy quality. When we receive God as a friend, we embrace one who is unpretentious and extremely approachable. We do not need to begin with a preface or disclaimers. Our words do not need to be perfectly constructed to be understood. He is an infinitely good friend. He knows our heart and intentions, and he still sticks around!

What is friendship? Without getting deep into the weeds, we can boil down friendship to one thing: company. A friend is someone who provides company—voluntary camaraderie. The etymology of the word *company* is interesting too.

with, together

Com pany

panis, meaning "bread"

Company is derived from two Latin words, indicating someone with whom you would share a meal.

Maybe Christ's famous words in Revelation 3:20 (as annotated at the start of this chapter) have more to do with friendship than we think!

Revelation 3:20 addresses the Laodiceans' lukewarm faith. Jesus invited the Laodiceans to repent and return to a vibrant relationship in which they might enjoy table fellowship with him. Our westernized culture treats meals casually. We grab food on the go, drink our breakfast, and throw a frozen pizza in the oven to eat in front of the TV. The biblical writers instead saw the table as a place of deep formation and intimacy.

In the ancient world, to share a meal was to share your life. Think about those friends who are so close and trusted that they are always welcome; maybe they even own a key to your house! The travesty of Revelation 3:20 is that Jesus had to knock to gain entrance to the Laodicean church, which should have already been in fellowship with him daily. The Laodiceans' stagnant faith caused them to miss out on friendship with Jesus. Christ wants to share life with us, not just a compartmentalized part of it.

Revelation 3:20 is the reminder that Jesus wants our welcoming hospitality. We did not initiate the relationship, but rather he asks for our friendship! He patiently, yet persistently, knocks on the door of our heart, wanting to reside there if we would make room for his awe-inspiring company. Don't wait until tomorrow to cherish the friendship he offers. After all, he's already at the door!

Do you hear him knocking?

WHAT DOES THIS MEAN FOR ME?

Our prayer life should be much more than a child's (fictitious) relationship with Santa Claus, in which the extent of the relationship is telling him what you want from him. **Prayer is engaging in the act of friendship with God.** And no one modeled this better than Jesus (see, for example, Mark 1:35; Luke 5:16; 6:12). Jesus, even though he was busy, had a lifestyle of prayer. From morning to evening he ministered to and served others. That can be exhausting! And what did he do when he had spare time? He prayed—he kept happy company with God. When are you going to keep company with God this week?

APPLY THIS: Pull out your calendar or phone right now. Schedule a recurring time with God on your calendar, and then show up for that intentional time of prayer.

11

God Is Our Protector

Psalm 121 (NLT)

I look up to the mountains—does my help come from there? My help comes

Psalm 146:5

from the LORD, who made heaven and earth! He will not let you

Hebrew verb: "to protect, guard"

stumble; the one who **watches** over you will not slumber. Indeed, he who **watches** over Israel never slumbers or sleeps. The LORD himself *watches* over you!

The LORD stands beside you as your *protective shade.* The sun will not harm you by day, nor the moon at night. The LORD *keeps*

Hebrew verb: "to protect, guard"

you from all harm and *watches* over your life. The LORD keeps *watch* over you as you come and go, both now and forever.

WHO HE IS

Isn't it funny how certain childhood fears seem to chase us into adulthood? Maybe you feared the dark—*and still do*. Oftentimes a significant other will have a hard time sleeping if their spouse is gone. There is something comforting about having each other during such a vulnerable time as sleep. Even the fiercest warriors drop their guard when their eyes shut for much-needed slumber. But who doesn't sleep? Our true protector and guardian—God. "Indeed, he who watches over Israel never slumbers or sleeps" (Ps. 121:4 NLT).

It is easy to take for granted the truth that God never needs to take naps. You might think, *Well, obviously he doesn't need sleep; he is God!* Let's recall, though, that Psalm 121 was written in ancient Israel, which was surrounded by pagan cultures with their own beliefs about various gods. For Israelites to believe that Yahweh (the Lord) "never slumbers or sleeps" was a unique truth, distinguishing him from other gods of the ancient Near East. The Babylonians, for example, had incantations or formulaic prayers for when a god was sleeping and not able to hear their prayers. Imagine trying to process that your prayer might be white noise to a sleepy, snoring deity. That's precisely why Elijah mocked Baal's prophets during their hours of prayer: "Cry aloud, for he is a god. Either he is musing, or he is relieving himself, or he is on a journey, or perhaps he is asleep and must be awakened" (1 Kings 18:27).

 **FUN FACT**

Jesus slept and even napped, because his human body needed rest (see Mark 4:38). However, this does not diminish the deity of Christ. In his incarnation, Jesus took on a true human nature while maintaining his deity. He became a genuine human being. This means that he could experience sensations such as tiredness and even sleep while still being God. But the exalted Lord no longer naps! He watches over us as he did thousands of years before his earthly ministry.

Before ancient Jews fell asleep, many would pray: "Blessed are you, Lord, our God, King of the Universe, who makes the bands of sleep fall upon my eyes, and slumber upon my eyelids." For them, sleep was recognized as a blessing from God, restoring the body and spirit! But for more than God's wakefulness, we should be enamored that he stands as our guardian and protector. The Hebrew verb for "protecting" (*šāmar*) appears five times in the eight brief verses of Psalm 121. This reveals a unique way in which God relates to us and cares for us.

No one can oblige God to look out for us. But God willingly "keeps watch over you as you come and go, both now and forever" (Ps. 121:8 NLT). God's guardian watch is as pervasive and enduring as his very existence. The verb for God's protection also appears in the famous Aaronic blessing:

"May the LORD bless you and protect you.
May the LORD smile on you and be gracious to you.
May the LORD show you his favor and give you his peace."

(NUM. 6:24–26 NLT)

Being in covenant relationship with God grants us his protection, which guards and preserves the blessed life he graciously gives. Therefore, he is not simply the protector of our life—whatever we make of it—but the protector of our life in relationship to him with the privileges and responsibilities he lavishes upon us.

 FUN FACT

A covenant relationship is a biblical concept involving God's promises. When God makes a covenant with people who trust him, it is a binding promise based on *his faithfulness* and *our response*.

WHAT DOES THIS MEAN FOR ME?

It's deeply encouraging to realize that God is our protector, but there are some caveats. The power of these verses is not that nothing perceivably bad will happen to us. Even the ancient Israelites would have had the common sense (and life experience!) to know that was *not* the case. God's care and protection are real, *even if* they don't take the shape we might hope or expect.

Consider Psalm 23:4: "Even though I walk through the valley of the shadow of death, I will fear no evil, for you are with me; your rod and your staff, they comfort me." A shepherd is a protector, responsible to guard and guide helpless sheep. Jesus alluded to himself as our shepherd (John 10). So Psalm 23 is teaching that even death cannot impede God's protection! He is our protector even through death; that's how faithful he is! We don't go around the dark valleys; he leads us through them (Ps. 23:4). And in the end, we traverse through death itself; so Jesus shepherds us even through death, since he knows the way through.

Jesus has made death a comma, not a period. He took what seemed to be the end and made it a new beginning. Our protector has been through death, so he can guard and guide us through that dark and mysterious unknown to life beyond the grave. He is a protector above and beyond anyone else in the world. "The LORD keeps watch over you as you come and go, both now and forever" (Ps. 121:8 NLT).

APPLY THIS: Read Numbers 6:24–26 as a blessing during times of fellowship with family or friends. If you have a family, try laying on hands and praying this blessing over them every evening before bed.

12

God Is Our Healer

IN A FLASH Faith isn't settling into suffering; it's fighting to see God as healer within it.

1 Peter 2:24

Jesus ·········

He himself bore our sins

in his body on the tree, that we

might die to sin and live

hanging on the cross by their hands and feet, they would die by suffocation ···········

to righteousness. By his wounds

past tense ············   ········ Isaiah 53:5

you have been healed.

············ to return back to a condition of
health or wholeness, unbroken
and undamaged

WHO HE IS

Through Christ's suffering and resurrection, God will heal all who believe.

Let's unpack that! God is restoring us back to our original, sinless, pure state—and even beyond, including an immortal resurrection body. He not only diagnoses but also treats the disease, paving the path to completion. As we live in the already-and-not-yet phase of salvation history, we have the opportunity to know God as healer and to reach out for his healing hand.

We may think of Christ's sacrifice on the cross as significant primarily for our souls, but it's just as transformative for our bodies and minds. Throughout Scripture, God healed people through demonic deliverance, alleviating illness and disease, and providing spiritual breakthrough. In Exodus 15:26, as God spoke to the Israelites, he told them, "I am the LORD, your healer." When speaking to a group of Jews living in Israel, he said, "I will restore health to you, and your wounds I will heal" (Jer. 30:17). Since God is the same yesterday, today, and forever, he is our healer too (Heb. 13:8).

ILLNESS OF SIN AND ETERNAL DEATH

Isa. 6:10, Isa. 53:5

Matt. 13:15, 1 Pet. 2:24

Matt. 28:16–20, 2 Cor. 5:11–21

God as Healer

PHYSICAL SICKNESS, DISEASE, OR DEATH

Ex. 21:19, 2 Kings 8:29

Matt. 4:23–24, Luke 8:47

Luke 9:1–2, 1 Cor. 12:9

MENTAL ILLNESS OR STRUGGLE

Ps. 18, Ps. 118:5

Matt. 9:35, Rev. 21:4

Luke 10:19, Eph. 6:10–18

DEMONIC POSSESSION AND OPPRESSION

Deut. 18:10–12, Isa. 61:1

Matt. 12:22, Luke 4:38–41

2 Cor. 10:3–4, 1 Pet. 5:8–9

● *Scripture in Old Testament*

● *Scripture in New Testament during Jesus's Ministry on Earth*

● *Scripture where God Ministers Healing through People*

In the Gospels, we read a story of a man who had leprosy, a contagious skin disease that attacks the nervous system, causing great pain and disfiguration (Mark 1:40–45). Under the Mosaic law, having such a skin disease meant a person was unclean and unwell.

In the first century, laws were set up to help stop the spread of this horrible disease. Often it spread through contact and from droplets from the upper respiratory system. That's why those with leprosy would be isolated, some for years, or sent to a leper colony. The family would steer clear of this person, often dropping off food and water by the door. Those with the disease would be banished from neighbors, family, and their community.

The leprous man Jesus spoke with quite possibly had not been touched, hugged, or even given a handshake for years. He had been cast aside, perhaps even forgotten, and was now pleading for both physical healing and social healing. Luke 5:12 says, "When he saw Jesus, he fell on his face and begged him, 'Lord, if you will, you can make me clean.'"

This man may have been sick, but he modeled a healthy theology of healing:

1. He knew Jesus as healer.

2. He pondered whether it was within Jesus's sovereignty and authority to heal him.

3. He reached out to Jesus for healing.

How did Jesus respond to this man who had been isolated and ostracized because of his highly contagious disease? **Jesus stretched out his hand and touched him.** He touched a man whom no one else would dare touch. God is so pure, powerful, and filled with compassion and love that, with just a touch, he cured the man of his leprosy, reversing decay and bringing physical healing.

Leviticus 13 says that if someone with leprosy had been healed and wanted to rejoin society, they had to be examined by a priest and receive a clean bill of health. The priest would then declare them clean or unclean. Jesus told the healed man to fulfill his obligation to go to the priest so he could rejoin society again—whole and healed. Jesus not only healed the man's sickness but also restored him to his community.

WHAT DOES THIS MEAN FOR ME?

To truly understand God as our healer, we must understand him as sovereign, powerful, and compassionate. There's a mystery of faith within unanswered pleas and wondering why God doesn't wave some magic wand and heal everyone who suffers. There are also false teachings that say you lack faith if you're still sick or suffering. Try telling that to Jesus's original disciples, who all suffered greatly and many were even murdered for their confessions of faith!

We will suffer even as we're in the process of full healing (1 Pet. 5:10). From illness to depression and everything in between, various hardships are not foreign to our humanity; they're rites of passage. These wrestling matches are often met with bigger questions to untangle. Does this mean if our bodies are physically ill, we settle into our diagnoses and never ask God for healing? No! Because we know God as healer, redeemer, and fixer of all the broken things, we have hope. As we wait and wonder, we continue to approach him for physical healing and for comfort while navigating the what-ifs and why-nots. From this posture, our prayers transform from "Why me?" to "Will you, Lord?"

At some point, our physical bodies will die and decay. *No amount of faith can change that fact.* Even after being brought back from the dead, Lazarus's physical body eventually lay lifeless again. Our faith continually reminds us that, even if God doesn't always seem to heal, he is still healer and is always leading his children through a redemptive healing process. The Bible declares God as healer even when we lack the eyes of faith to see or understand the *process* of healing.

 FUN FACT

Within the original biblical text, in both Hebrew and Greek, there are various terms that describe the act of healing. "In Hebrew, the most common words for healing come from the root *rāpā'* ('to heal'), which describes a process of restoration to a state of well-being or wholeness."[10]

Divine healing points us to Christ, removes obstacles in sharing the gospel, and provides us with opportunities to support others. In the places of waiting, **Holy Spirit** equips and empowers Christ followers to reach out for healing for others too! He moves through people with gifts of healing (1 Cor. 12:9). Both of us (Brayden and Jenny) have experienced firsthand instances of God bringing healing to others, freeing them from lupus, years of back pain, and demonic oppression. We know he still heals. Jesus brought restoration through those significant moments of ministry, and he gets the glory today too!

Are you in a season of suffering or hoping for healing? Remember, Jesus is restoring the whole person—spiritually, physically, mentally, emotionally, and socially. There's wholeness for you, as God invites you into healing that can happen in an instant or through a process. Yet even in the process of waiting for healing, may your mind and heart remember that God is a promise keeper and he is who he says he is.

When our circumstances scream otherwise, may we be so tenacious to know and experience God as healer. At the end of the day, we will all experience God's total healing power through resurrection—and death, decay, disease, and fatigue will have no place in our newfound eternal lives! That hope anchors us amid the victories and disappointments of this life.

God's children will be healed and whole. May our faith be so bold that even within our brokenness in the waiting, we share a similar desperation as the man who was sick with leprosy. We know Jesus as healer, we wonder if it's within his sovereignty and authority, and we reach out to him for healing. From this posture, miracles are witnessed.

APPLY THIS: Today, pray for healing for yourself, or pray with someone in need of healing.

God Is Our Rabbi

 IN A FLASH Discipleship is a journey of walking bravely with our Rabbi, being taught by him and becoming like him.

Matthew 4:18-22

While walking by the Sea

Jesus ┄┄┄┄┄

of Galilee, |he| *saw two brothers,*

Simon (who is called Peter) and

Andrew his brother, casting a net into

the sea, for they were fishermen.

he says to them ┄┄┄┄┄

And he said to them, **"Follow me,**

and I will make you fishers of men."

Immediately they left their nets

┄┄┄┄┄ *Without delay*

and *followed him.* *And going*

on from there he saw two other

brothers, James the son of Zebedee

and John his brother, in the boat

with Zebedee their father, mending

their nets, and he called them.

Immediately they left the boat and

their father and followed him.

All of our discipleship journeys are a response to hearing Jesus say, "Follow me." Maybe we read this invitation in the Gospels or heard someone tell us that Jesus wants us to follow him! Sadly, it seems that "following Jesus" has become meaningless jargon, just another way of saying you're a Christian. While Christians are those who follow Jesus, there are unique angles of talking about how we relate to Jesus. So what does it mean to *follow* Jesus in real life?

WHO HE IS

FUN FACT

The word *rabbi* comes from the Hebrew language and is a way for a student to refer to their teacher or master. It is both a term of endearment and a term of respect.

Before Jesus made his deity explicitly clear to the world, he announced himself as a rabbi who was eager to take on students. That was what rabbis did; they taught their students how to become like *them*. The person you called "rabbi" was the person whose example you were determined to follow! It was a big deal who you chose to be your rabbi, since your life's devotion was to walk, talk, and pray like them. Disciples imitate their rabbi—and Christians are no exception. Jesus is our rabbi, and a primary goal of our discipleship is to become like him. "A disciple is not above his teacher, but everyone when he is fully trained will be like his teacher" (Luke 6:40).

What Did Jesus Teach?

Based on the Gospels, what might we identify as Jesus's central teaching? What was Rabbi Jesus's favorite topic to talk about at length? While many seem to think that Jesus spoke about hell more than any other topic, that's not the case. The word for *hell* appears only eleven times in the Synoptic Gospels. Clearly, hell is not the center or main way

IMPORTANT THINGS RABBI JESUS TAUGHT IN THE SYNOPTIC GOSPELS (MATTHEW, MARK, LUKE)

GREEK WORD	TOPIC	NUMBER OF TIMES MENTIONED
basileia	Kingdom	121
aphiēmi	Forgiveness	50
proseuchomai	Prayer	44
patēr	Father	42
pisteuō	Faith	34
geenna	Hell	11

the New Testament talks about sin and salvation. In reality, the topic Jesus taught most about in the Gospels was the kingdom! This shows that Christ's priority as a rabbi was to teach people about the kingdom of God and how to live by kingdom priorities.

So while Jesus was teaching, healing, multiplying wine, walking on water, and everything else he did—his primary objective was to teach kingdom principles. Jesus was not only focused on raising up disciples with good morals, he was also crafting citizens of a new society. He was training up people who would be welcomed into his kingdom and reign with him in a new and profound way that the world had not seen.

Consider who Jesus originally called to be his disciples. He didn't exactly start out with the holy-rollers all-star team of his day. At least four were fishermen, Matthew was a tax collector (considered a traitor to his own people), and Simon the Zealot was, well, a Zealot—meaning he was trained in guerrilla warfare to fight the Romans. He must have been surprised by Christ's peaceful methods.

Speaking of Peter and John (formerly fishermen), Acts 4:13 says, "Now when they [the religious leaders] saw the boldness of Peter and John, and perceived that they were uneducated, common men, they were astonished. And they recognized that they had been with Jesus." The original disciples were common people with an uncommon ministry because they were companions of Christ. Can people in our lives tell by our actions that we have "been with Jesus"? Following Jesus means being with him. Learning from our rabbi means emulating his way of life.

Jesus called people as they were, and all were works in progress. Consider your own story. Do you feel like you have some gaps in your spiritual formation? We do too. But Jesus doesn't ask us to follow him *only after* meeting certain prerequisites. Instead, he asks, like he did with the disciples in Matthew 4:18–22, that we drop everything and follow him. No prerequisites, no entrance exams, no starting bar—just come as you are, where you are. In this sense, anyone can become a disciple of Rabbi Jesus (*and that's kind of the point!*). But there is that one caveat: you must drop everything to follow him. **Following Rabbi Jesus involves abandoning your former way of life to form a new identity as his disciple.**

Matthew tells us that Jesus was "walking by the sea" (Matt. 4:18), which might seem insignificant, but where else would Jesus find fishermen such as Peter, Andrew, James, and John? Assuming Jesus truly intended for these men to be his disciples, he had to find them where they were. Does Jesus not do this with us? We don't go searching for Jesus; he goes searching for us!

The Greek text of Matthew 4:19 has two gems in it. First, the narrator's comment "he said to them" is actually in the present tense in Greek ("he *says* to them"). One of the reasons for the present tense in a historical narrative is to make the narrative vivid, drawing us into the text, as if we too were on the beach that day.[11] It's like Matthew wants us to hear Jesus speaking to us directly. Second, verse 19 says, "Follow me," which in Greek reads like a proclamation, not a proposal. Rather than laying out options on the table, Jesus captivated those men on the beach and implored them to reorient their whole lives around him. "Immediately," Peter and Andrew (his brother) "left their nets and followed him" (Matt. 4:20). John and James did the same: "Immediately they left the boat and their father and followed him" (v. 22).

The early readers of Matthew's gospel understood the sacrifice these men made. They gave up a stable, albeit modest, career to support their families and a predictable pattern of life *for ... what exactly*? Their future, following their rabbi, was a journey into the unknown. What would their lives become? It was indeed a mystery to them, but they were sure it was worth it—whatever this *it* would turn out to be. The disciples were called as they were, where they were, never to remain the same. Could we follow Rabbi Jesus with such simplicity of faith?

WHAT DOES THIS MEAN FOR ME?

All of this might sound overwhelming. Can we really become like Jesus—walk like him, talk like him, even exemplify him? It's easier (in our opinion) to trust him for salvation than to follow him with the aim of becoming like him. But who are we to question Jesus for calling us as his disciples? Although we (accurately) see ourselves as projects in need of total renovation (watch out, *Extreme Makeover*), our God is the ultimate architect and devotes himself to the task!

As our Savior, Jesus secured our salvation apart from our ability or effort *(praise the Lord!)*. As our rabbi, though, following Jesus is an *active* and *ongoing* response, fueled by Holy Spirit. Being Spirit-filled is all about personifying the teachings and presence of Jesus in the world, because the Spirit of Jesus is alive in us and moves through us. That is why the Christians were first called *Christians*—because they were *Christ-like*.

 **FUN FACT**

In Romans 8:9, Paul referred to Holy Spirit as "the Spirit of Christ" to show that the presence of Christ in the world was now residing in and through Christians.

Many of us want to experience the joy of Jesus without putting on the mantle of Jesus. We all want God's peace, but are we willing to adopt his priorities? Are we guilty of wanting an adventurous faith without any sacrifice? **When it comes to following Jesus, the reward is in the work.** It's like a photographer who wants the best photos of the sunrise. Capturing the sunrise requires waking up early; the reward is in the experience of being up in time to see it.

What would happen if we had a radical reorientation of our lives like the original disciples did? What if we, so to speak, dropped our nets and left our boats? It's not a matter of quitting our jobs tomorrow or moving across the world. He will lead us in what to do, which will look slightly different for each of us. But the common core for all Christians is this—to follow him with empty hands and open hearts.

"Follow me," Jesus says.

Your move.

APPLY THIS: Read "The Great Commission" found in Matthew 28:16–20. What is Jesus our rabbi challenging us to see as our responsibility? What promise does he give as encouragement? Journal about this.

14

God Is Our Liberator

IN A FLASH The cost of true freedom was paid by the blood of Jesus, conquering sin and the spiritual powers that enslaved us.

Luke 4:17-19

The scroll of the prophet Isaiah was given to him. Jesus *He unrolled the scroll and found the place where* Isaiah 61:1–2 *it was written, "The Spirit of the Lord is upon me, because he has anointed me to proclaim good news to the poor. He has sent me to proclaim* liberty *to the* captives

and recovering of sight to the blind,

to set at liberty *those who are*

oppressed, *to* proclaim *the year*

of the Lord's favor."

Psalm 146:7

spiritual blindness, see Acts 26:18

Isaiah 58:6

WHO HE IS

The theme of freedom from slavery weaves in and out of the Old Testament. In Exodus, the Israelites were slaves in Egypt. God equipped Moses to contend for their independence, so he approached Egypt's Pharaoh about setting them free. His refusal resulted in God bringing about ten torturous plagues. The last plague involved God killing the firstborn of every household in Egypt. The Israelites, however, marked their doors with the blood of a lamb as an indication of faith in God, so that the angel of God would spare their firstborns, having the angel pass over their homes *(get it, the Passover?)*.

After his own son was found dead, Pharaoh finally relented and let the Israelites go. Later, Moses said to the newly freed Israelites, "Remember this day in which you came out from Egypt, out of the house of slavery, for by a strong hand the LORD brought you out from this place" (Ex. 13:3). While the ten plagues might seem like a battle between Moses and Pharaoh, it was really a battle between Yahweh, the God of Israel, and the so-called gods of Egypt. Each plague demonstrated Yahweh's mastery over nature, mocking the claims about the Egyptian gods. The climactic killing of the Egyptians' firstborn sons demonstrated that Yahweh was the true author of life. As a whole, the Exodus narrative shows that Yahweh is the almighty master of the universe, and when he wants to liberate his people, no one—not even the gods of the world's most powerful kingdoms—can stop him!

A lot of work went into securing this freedom. The problem was that it was temporary. As time went on, the Israelites found themselves enslaved again and again—to other empires, sure, but even more to sin and the powers of darkness (demonic powers or false gods).

FUN FACT

The word *liberty* comes from the Greek word *aphesis*, which is a verb meaning "to release," "forgive," or "set free," depending on context. It indicates the state of having a particular obligation removed in a given relationship.

After God established a covenant with Moses on Mount Sinai (Ex. 19–24), he continually reminded his people to obey the law. The covenant was conditional; when they obeyed the law, God provided blessing and they were set apart in the land (Deut. 28). To disobey would reap consequences. Shocker, the children of Israel did not keep their end of the covenant agreement. They worshipped idols, and their sinfulness showed their need for a Savior. In a surprising turn of events, the God who delivered them from Egypt delayed their entry into the Promised Land because of their lack of faith exercised through disobedience. During this wilderness season, the Israelites longed to go back to the land of Egypt, *even back into slavery.* They craved (false) comfort of the familiar past at the expense of the new blessing God was inviting them into.

ROAD TO FREEDOM

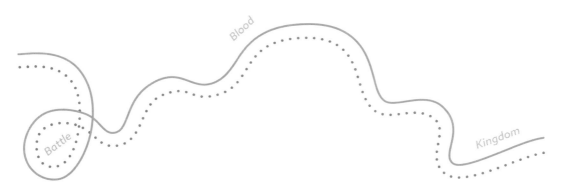

Comes by means of God defeating the powers of Egypt through the plagues (Ex. 6:6)	Unifies the people under a covenant sealed with blood (Ex. 24:8)	Declared to be heirs of the Promised Land (Ex. 12:25)
Comes by means of Jesus defeating the powers of darkness through the death and resurrection (Col. 1:13–20)	Unifies the people under a new covenant sealed with blood (1 Cor. 11:25)	Declared to be heirs of the promised new world (Rom. 8:16–25)

· · · *First Exodus (Temporary)*

— *New Exodus (Enduring)*

But that's not the end of the story; with God, it never is. The Israelites' quest for freedom served as a pattern for an even greater exodus to come. The Old Testament pointed toward Israel's Messiah and the permanent freedom given through him to his chosen people. They didn't work for this freedom by being right or following all the rules per se; rather, the free gift of forgiveness set them free.

Jesus paid the ultimate sacrifice: his life. God's children were marked by the blood of the Lamb. His blood delivered them from the plagues of sin and death and brought them into abundant life. He is the true Passover Lamb (1 Cor. 5:7). Paul wrote:

> For one who has died has been **set free** from sin. Now if we have died with Christ, we believe that we will also live with him. We know that Christ, being raised from the dead, will never die again; **death no longer has dominion** over him. For the death he died he died to sin, once for all, but the life he lives he lives to God. So you also **must** consider yourselves dead to sin and alive to God in Christ Jesus. (Rom. 6:7–11)

Nothing else has the authority or power to liberate us in this way—nothing but Jesus. **Christ is our liberator, providing us the freedom to speak, behave, move, and think beyond the constraints of death, sin, shame, and the schemes of the enemy.**

WHAT DOES THIS MEAN FOR ME?

The apostle Peter reminded Christians to "live as free people, but do not use your freedom as a cover-up for evil; live as God's slaves" (1 Pet. 2:16 NIV). True freedom means abiding in and belonging to the triune God—which sounds counterintuitive. This freedom is not for selfish gain but fueled from the love of a Savior. Slaves simply obey the commands of their masters. But our obedience is fueled by love—for it is far easier to obey someone you love!

Think of freedom like a rescue dog. Imagine a dog chained in a yard and abandoned. She is unprotected, and she can't escape or find the nourishment she needs to live a healthy life. She needs to be rescued.

The rescue crew arrives, then frees her from her chain and gives her a new name: Freedom. At her new home, Freedom stays close to her master, as she's tethered to a leash. But the leash feels different from the chain that once bound her. Freedom has space to move and the comfort and companionship of her master. She's given an entire yard to move and play in. The master even builds a fence around the yard, providing a safe environment against predators. Freedom is experiencing protection.

When Freedom is alone, though, she doesn't act free. She sits in one place, almost as if she's chained up again. She forgets the experiences of walking with her master, the voice that calls "Come," and the friendly hands that provide nourishment and direction. The rain comes, and Freedom gets dirty; thunder strikes, and she is scared. Shelter and protection are available to her, but she still sits as if she's in chains. Will she live up to her name and truly be free? Will Freedom roam and explore? Will she seek shelter when she needs it? Or will she remain stuck, feeling disregarded or forgotten, and place herself in paralyzing shackles?

God has entrusted you with space to freely roam the earth, while heeding his calls to come and worship him. He is teaching you how to move in the safety and protection of knowing him. **The most significant way you can express your freedom is by being enslaved to your liberator—Christ.** You are bound to the Lord, belonging to him, ultimately for your betterment. God has given you a fence with boundaries and a yard to roam. But God's boundaries are never to restrict his blessings; they are to protect the blessed life he desires for you (see Ps. 16:5–6)! These boundaries funnel you toward greener pastures. May your actions, motives, and heart desires fall under the authority of Scripture and within the understanding of who Christ is.

No one who acts as if the chains are still there is truly free. The Israelites craved being put back in chains. Just like the dog Freedom—and many Christians—we can easily and inadvertently chain ourselves back up. The false freedoms of the world cause destruction and doubt. But Christ died so we can be free of false comforts, addictions, the need for accolades, and the entanglements of sin.

Whether you express your freedom or not, you are still free. Just as John 8:36 says, "If the Son sets you free, you will be free indeed." The instant you met Christ, those chains were unlocked, and an invitation awaited—an invitation to intimacy with the Liberator. He's invited you to run, to worship, to contend for his promises, to speak his truth, to love others well, and to boldly strengthen the Church through your spiritual giftings. This freedom gives you authority for him! Are you experiencing the true freedom of walking with your master? Live free, Christ follower. God is with you. Indeed, you are free.

Your chains have been broken, but have you walked out of the cell?

APPLY THIS: Display freedom today by demonstrating an act of boldness through serving. Reach out to a stranger, friend, or fellow church member. Pray with them, send them an encouraging card, or make or buy them a meal. Trust God to freely move through your time together.

15

God Is Our Guide

IN A FLASH Holy Spirit advocates for us and guides us through our faith journey.

John 16:13-14

John 14:17

When the Spirit of truth comes,

Holy Spirit/the helper, see John 14:26

he will guide you into all the

truth, **for he will not speak on his**

certainty   *Holy Spirit*

own authority, but whatever he hears

he will speak, and he will declare to

you the things that are to come.

Christ follower   *Jesus*

He will glorify me, for he will take

Holy Spirit   *Jesus*   *Holy Spirit*

what is mine and declare it to you.

Sometimes being directly challenged feels like a curse. Imagine it's dusk and you're driving to visit some friends at their new house in a rural area. The roads winding through the woods aren't well marked and your phone reception has given out. You end up repeating the same turns, like a dog chasing his tail. When you can't find your bearings, you just continue to move in circles. There's no map in your car, because MapQuest was so ten years ago. Alone in the darkness with a can of Pringles and the inability to navigate to their house, you realize you are utterly lost.

Before we met Christ, spiritual darkness clung to us. We probably thought we knew where we were going, but we were headed in the wrong direction. We couldn't find our place in this journey of life. Whether we realized it or not, our navigation tools were broken. Without a working compass, GPS, map, or guide, we were lost. "Turn left. Turn left. Turn left." Our broken navigation system had us spinning in circles. *What job should I get? Where should I live? Who do I marry? Why am I overwhelmed all the time? How do I help my child find joy again?* We followed that gut feeling, intuition, or perhaps some type of moral compass; created a set of ethics based on our experience; and used common sense through writing a pro/con list. These tools aren't necessarily bad, but they can mislead us, because they only allow us to see in part.

Trusting solely in a gut feeling is flawed because humanity is flawed. Apart from God, we are lost—with faulty navigation tools and made-up truths.

WHO HE IS

In knowing Christ, we become born again, made new (2 Cor. 5:17). This is regeneration. We see God's goodness, and our soul (containing our mind, will, and emotions) is awakened to new life. Our soul then begins to participate in this divine nature. We start to walk as sons and daughters who bear the image of their Father and know they are set apart. This is sanctification. We desire to be aligned with the will of God and his mission. And we are given a set of navigation tools to do just that. Through Christ, we're connected to the Spirit of God by the indwelling of Holy Spirit, making us a mobile temple of God's presence (1 Cor. 3:16).

In John 16:13–14, Jesus was preparing his disciples for his departure. He told them he would send Holy Spirit, the Paraclete (John 14:16, 26; 15:26; 16:7).

Holy Spirit is also our advocate. He's our helper, compass, and guide. **Holy Spirit guides us down the path toward the richness and revelation of Jesus.** Like a compass, the Spirit leads us on the only way to eternal life, and it's through the Son, Jesus (John 14:6). As we continue to walk in faith and journey closer to God, Holy Spirit continues to convict us, change us, and set our feet on the right path.

Have you ever used a GPS but zoomed in so close to the map that you only saw a few feet in front of you? You can't see when the next turn will be or what direction you'll go next. When you zoom out the GPS, the full picture of the journey makes sense. You see the hills, valleys, rough terrain, smooth roads, twists, and turns to get to the final destination. When we rely solely on human instinct, it's like trying to navigate with a zoomed-in GPS. We are limited by our human abilities. But when we rely on Holy Spirit, we trust the one who sees the entire map in great detail. God is the author of this story, and he knows how to lead you to his kingdom.

WHAT DOES THIS MEAN FOR ME?

It's hard to trust when you can only see a few feet in front of you. But with Holy Spirit indwelling you, you finally have a reliable navigation system. You can trust the one guiding and leading you. Respond to Holy Spirit's promptings as he continually points you to Jesus.

Psalm 25:5 says, "Lead me in your truth and teach me, for you are the God of my salvation; for you I wait all the day long." Learning to follow the lead of Holy Spirit takes time. It's a learned discipline that requires practice and patience. That is why the apostle Paul used phrases like "keep in step with the Spirit" (Gal. 5:25).

We can compare being led by the Spirit to following our trusty navigation system in the car. We receive directions, but it's up to us to pay attention and move as instructed. We have to rise above any distractions to hear the voice directing us and then put our foot on the gas and drive as instructed. It's simply listening and responding. It takes us putting our foot on the pedal to move, but it doesn't take our initiative. We are already being led, and it's our responsibility to follow the guidance.

Hearing the guide and trusting enough to go where it says are two different things. We can sometimes be tempted to create our own route because we think we know better or we want to arrive faster. Then we end up with a manufactured, human-made route. We may find our own way, but speaking from experience, it's most often a painful process that leads to a dead end or spinning in circles and the need for repentance. The beautiful thing about taking the scenic route with God is that he's always along for the ride; we just need to be attentive and responsive to his guidance.

HOW DO YOU TRUST AND UNDERSTAND GOD'S BEST DIRECTION FOR YOUR LIFE?

Remember these things:

As you learn to navigate life with God, it gets more natural to hear and recognize his voice over time.

You'll boldly see God's power manifest through you. Holy Spirit has given believers supernatural giftings to strengthen the common good of the Church (1 Cor. 12; Heb. 2:4).

Holy Spirit is your guide.

You'll begin to see signposts of his presence in your life. Godly character like love, joy, peace, patience, kindness, goodness, faithfulness, gentleness, and self-control will move within you (Gal. 5:22–23). These may also serve as indicators that God is leading!

Wise counsel may also guide you (Prov. 11:14). This is why it's imperative to be in a local Bible-teaching church or seek out biblical counseling when applicable.

God's Word may also give you direction (Ps. 119:105). We must discern God's will within the authority of Scripture and his character.

The journey can be a beautiful, enjoyable ride. Keep running the race God has for you. You don't have to figure it out on your own. Keep in step with the Spirit, and let God lead!

APPLY THIS: Make a "gratitude list" of all the ways God has guided you and directed your steps over the last few weeks. As you pause to reflect on God, take time to celebrate the very nature of who he is!

16

God Is Our Spouse

IN A FLASH Redemption is a romance where the Lord Jesus takes his people as his bride.

Ephesians 5:31-32

Quoting Genesis 2:24

"Therefore a man shall leave his father and mother and hold fast to

the metaphor

his wife, and the two shall become

an idiom for marriage

one flesh." This mystery is

once concealed, now revealed

profound, and I am saying that it

marriage

refers to Christ and the church.

Christians individually and collectively   *the reality*

WHO HE IS

Many months go into planning it. The days leading up to it build anticipation. And yet, the day flies by with an inversion of time that feels surreal. Weddings are some of the most sacred days, regardless of one's religious background. With the moments speeding by even faster than a camera can capture, one thing is always in frame for a photographer—the face of the groom as his bride walks down the aisle. There she is, stunning. And although friends and family are there to celebrate the occasion, the groom loses sight of everyone and everything, eyes locked on to her. But his vision isn't so keen for long, for tears breach the surface and the subtle smell of salt drips down his cheeks. It is pure euphoria, an incorruptible moment. Lost in a singular vision of love, a bride and a groom make their way until they stand, hand in hand, ready to begin life anew under a singular identity, bound by the sharing of a family name.

What if weddings pointed to something more ultimate than two people exchanging vows? What if weddings somehow anticipated something more *real*? Yep, you read that right. No more hypotheticals. Marriage is a metaphor for the gospel. And our Lord looks at the Church with the groom's eyes on his wedding day.

Ephesians 5:31–32 follows on the coattails of Paul's instruction to husbands and wives. Heading toward the pinnacle of his point, Paul quoted Genesis 2:24, about Adam and Eve's marriage. Paul stated that "this mystery" of marriage is about Christ and the church (Eph. 5:32). In essence, marriage is a type, a signpost even, pointing toward the marriage of which all marriages are a shadow: Jesus marrying his covenant people. This is key—marriage of husband and wife is the metaphor, not the real thing. Christ joined with the Church is the reality of marriage. It is not a cute sermon illustration for earthly marriage, but just the reverse! Think about it this way: the ideal marriage, found at the beginning of the Bible in Eden, was still not the ultimate aim of marital love. Because one day, marriage will become about the Messiah marrying his bride whom he rescued with his own blood.

The whole story of redemption is peppered with passages that reinforce this idea, making it a climactic theme with the coming of the Messiah.

And I will betroth you to me forever.

I will betroth you to me in **righteousness**

and in **justice**, in steadfast **love** and in **mercy**.

I will betroth you to me in **faithfulness**.

And you shall know the LORD.

(HOS. 2:19–20)

Betrothal language sounds so lofty and Shakespearean. However, this could very well be translated as: "I will take you to be my spouse forever." Being betrothed is not synonymous with being engaged. Engagements nowadays are just a verbal commitment and nothing more. Back in biblical days, betrothals were commitments as serious and binding as marriage, minus the formal ceremony and consummation. So the Lord's promise to take his people as his bride is not an empty one, like that of the friend who got engaged multiple times without a marriage. All who trust in Christ will be given this highest privilege of a spouse relationship, the collective Church together becoming the bride of the Creator himself.

Hosea 2:19–20 references a custom of the day, which was to pay a bride-price or dowry to obtain the bride. In this case, the Lord gives righteousness, justice, steadfast love, and mercy as the price to purchase his beloved. God's righteousness, not our own, qualifies the marriage.

"You shall know the LORD" (Hos. 2:20) intentionally uses the verb "know" (*yada* in Hebrew), which signifies *an intimate kind of knowledge.* In the same way, this is what the Lord thinks of you. He desires to know you and be known in a way that can only be described with marital-type knowledge.

The Lord's intensity and passion within Hosea 2:19–20 are shown by using "betroth" three times. And while this passage appears in the Old Testament, the context makes it apparent that this was something new, though always intended. Marital love is the kind of love that embodies the new covenant and the people of God. And this is now realized by the arrival of Jesus. No wonder Paul saw the whole Bible as leading to a theology of the Lord as the bridegroom!

Paul even saw his position of "singleness" as advantageous (1 Cor. 7). In our sex-obsessed culture, we need this reminder from Paul; we are not any more or less whole because of our earthly marital status. Further, beyond any love we could receive through the love of any marriage, the Lord intends to pour out a kind of love that surpasses any we could ever receive. And that's why Paul also used the language of being "one spirit" with the Lord: "But he who is joined to the Lord becomes one spirit with him" (1 Cor. 6:17). This is a kind of union that categorically transcends any we can find in human relationships. There is a oneness with the Lord in "spirit" that can only be described through these sorts of metaphors, to where we belong to the Lord in a relationship of togetherness and love.

So if we full-circle back to Ephesians 5:31–32 where we started this chapter, we can see how Paul took a cover-to-cover approach to marriage. The first Eden was for Adam and his bride; the final Eden will be for Christ and his bride. How our Lord can love us so individually yet collectively is a mystery to us, and that is okay. If Jesus could sustain the stars in place, we can trust that he can satisfy our longing for love. **After all, marriage is no longer a metaphor when it is with Jesus; it is the goal of why we were created.**

The whole story of creation and new creation would be incomplete without the wedding between Christ the Lord and his beloved Church. Revelation 19:6–9 foretells of the return of Christ as a wedding: "for the marriage of the Lamb has come" (v. 7). The God of infinite love desires to make a bride out of us, his redeemed people, and reign with us forevermore. The gospel is the greatest love story ever told!

WHAT DOES THIS MEAN FOR ME?

Every person who finds themselves united to Jesus is not *only* united to their Savior for salvation but also united to him in the most loving union. The loyal love of Jesus is the authentic expression of the covenant of marriage. At this point in the redemptive story, we are "betrothed" to Christ the Lord, but the wedding has not yet come. Part of the excitement involving the return of the Lord is the fact that he comes to marry his bride and reign in the new creation. Since the full benefits and effects of that are still approaching, we wait with eager anticipation for the picture painted in Revelation 19:6–9.

Charles Spurgeon said it well: **"Those who are married to Jesus will be endlessly happy."[12] Christ takes the collective Church as his bride, resulting in a happy union that can only be metaphorically compared to marriage.** And so, the biblical story of redemption is a story of romance. It is not merely one we read about, but one we are invited into. Jesus spoke vows over the Church and said "I do." Instead of dropping to a knee to propose, the Lord willingly took up the cross. It was not a ring in his hand, but nails. Jesus sets us free, but not for blank-page liberation. He ransoms us for romance's sake. He offers us his very unveiled heart. Do you receive it? If so, don't be afraid to say "I do."

APPLY THIS: Pray about the significance of the Church being the bride of Christ. Is the Lord your source of love even beyond what a spouse could provide?

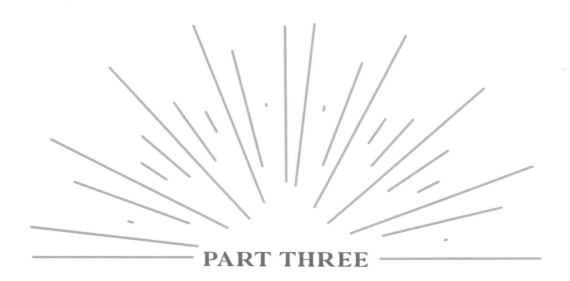

PART THREE

WHAT IS GOD LIKE?

The last part of this book dives deeper into the heart of God. Asking "What is God like?" is another way of asking about his heart or his character. These character traits or attributes of God were selectively chosen, and many more could be added as we continue to consider what God is like! However, our hope is that this will serve to connect your heart to his, both in receiving God's love, mercy, and grace and also in embodying these characteristics as God's image bearers.

17

God Pursues Us

IN A FLASH God seeks after us even when we are hiding from him.

Genesis 3:1-10

*Now the serpent was more crafty than any other beast of the field that the L*ORD *God had made. He said to the woman, "Did God actually say,*

.... *They were allowed to eat of any of the trees except one!*

'You shall not eat of any tree in the garden'?" And the woman said to the serpent, "We may eat of the fruit of

the trees in the garden, but God said, 'You shall not eat of the fruit of the tree that is in the midst of the garden, neither shall you touch it, lest you die.'" But the serpent said to the woman, "You will not surely die. For God knows that when you eat of it your eyes will be opened, and you will be like God, knowing good and

.... Adam and Eve were already like God, made in his image (Gen. 1:26–27).

evil." So when the woman saw that the tree was good for food, and that it was a delight to the eyes, and that the tree was to be desired to make one wise, she took of its fruit and ate, and she also gave some to her husband who was with her, and he ate. Then the eyes of both were opened, and they knew that they were naked. And they sewed fig leaves together and made themselves loincloths.

And they heard the sound of

Nakedness symbolized their vulnerability. While it is a good thing to be vulnerable, sin entered in to distort it.

the Lord God walking in the garden in the cool of the day, and the man and his wife hid themselves from the presence of the Lord God among the trees of the garden. But the Lord God called to the man and said to him, "Where are you?" And he said, "I heard the sound of you in the garden, and I was afraid, because I was naked, and I hid myself."

Sin caused humans to hide from God.

Beyond the strange and exotic (like a talking snake), something paramount about God's heart was on full display during humanity's trajectory-changing moment, known as the fall, when Adam and Eve, on behalf of all humanity, tainted the human condition with sin. What do we see of God's heart here? Let's imagine that life is like a game of hide-and-seek. If the characters are God and humanity, then who is the one doing the hiding and who is the one doing the seeking?

WHAT HE IS LIKE

Genesis 3:9 records the Lord saying, "Where are you?" It's a profound question with layers to it. Where am I? Sitting at home, why? Or is the question asking something more existential? If the fall of Adam and Eve tells us anything about human nature, it's this: We hide from God. He doesn't hide from us. **The Bible is the story of God seeking humanity, not the other way around.**

Religions try to tell you how to get to God. The Bible tells us how God comes to us. God asks, "Where are you?" What a question coming from the God who is omniscient! The God who knows all asks, with sincerity, "Where are you?" By putting this question out there, he gives us a chance to respond by vocalizing our vulnerability. We get a chance to call out that we have lost our way. And he chases us.

God's pursuit of humanity climaxed in the incarnation, when Jesus drew so near to us as being Yahweh in the flesh—God incarnate—having come to seek us out and save us. Then the conversation moved from "Where are you?" to "Follow me." But our Lord did not end with giving us instruction. It wasn't "Follow me, and do this and that." Nope. Rather our Lord said, "Follow me, and you will see how I will ultimately solve the problem stemming back to Genesis 3." And what did he do? He sacrificed his life. His life was a gift to us and the reason why he was born.

But let's just talk about the death of Christ for a moment. As Christians, we believe Jesus's death covers our sins. This is also known as "atonement." But where did atonement begin? Not with Mosaic law. The idea of God covering our sins started back in Genesis 3.

Kāpar

Hebrew verb for *atonement*.

Means "covering." It's the idea of having a wrong erased by
placing a covering over it. Although this word does not
appear in Genesis 3, the concept is present.

Look again at what Adam and Eve did in Genesis 3:7: "Then the eyes of both of them were opened, and they knew they were naked; so they sewed fig leaves together and made coverings for themselves" (CSB). When they realized they were naked—exposed and vulnerable—they tried to cover themselves. Isn't that what we do? We try to cover ourselves up and make sin seem like it hasn't affected us that much. But who are we fooling?

What are the "fig leaves" you cover yourself with? What ways do you try to make yourself seem more put together? It seems that Genesis 3 is a microcosm of everyday life.

Shame was not part of the fabric of God's original creation. It is one of the byproducts of sin. Instead of allowing ourselves to be spiritually "naked" before God, we cover ourselves, putting on such a charade that many of us even trick ourselves into believing the lie. But the story didn't end there. And although God announced the dreadful reality that sin brought into the world, he also introduced the hope of one who would crush the serpent. Genesis 3:15 contains this announcement, known as the *protoeuangelion*, which means "first gospel," because it was the first time anyone heard the good news of someone coming to reverse the curse of sin.

Genesis 3:21 reads, "And the LORD God made for Adam and for his wife garments of skins and clothed them." If God covered Adam and Eve, he first stripped them of the coverings they had made. He removed the facade and came face to face with their condition—the reality of who they were even after their self-awareness was exposed.

God personally covered them. That he covered them with "garments of skins" means an animal was sacrificed for them. This is the first example of atonement. But all forms of sacrifice and atonement in the biblical narrative lacked fulfillment until Christ, the true Passover Lamb, was sacrificed. Then, suddenly, there was no longer any need to be covered, because the Messiah had covered us by his own blood (1 Cor. 5:7).

Isaiah 61:10 says what God covered us with: "I will greatly rejoice in the LORD; my soul shall exult in my God, for he has clothed me with the garments of salvation; he has covered me with the robe of righteousness, as a bridegroom decks himself like a priest with a beautiful headdress, and as a bride adorns herself with her jewels."

As Isaiah prophesied gospel truths that would come to fulfillment in Christ, he said that God is the one who clothes and covers us. We are clothed "with the garments of salvation" and covered "with the robe of righteousness." Salvation and righteousness are not realities we strive for; they are gifts we receive from the greatest gift giver of all time.

Note also that the Hebrew verb for "clothed" in Isaiah 61:10 ("he has clothed me") is the same verb used in Genesis 3:21 ("the LORD ... clothed them"). God has been in the business of clothing and covering ever since the fall in Genesis 3. And the product of his clothing and covering is salvation and righteousness.

This is the story of the fall of humanity. And amid the great tragedy, we see something of the great grace of God, that he is the one who pursues us. If this is a game of hide-and-seek, he is the one calling out, "Ready or not, here I come!" We may hide from God, but he does not hide from us. And he does not want to play this game forever. Our separation from God is self-inflicted. Like Adam and Eve, we are the ones who place ourselves in hiding.

God is calling out, "Where are you?" And so, we ask, "Where are you?"

Are you covering yourself in some facade of fig leaves? Or are you allowing God to find you just as you are? There is no reason to fear calling out to God, "Here I am." You might even say, "Here I am. I feel broken, confused, hurt, betrayed, shame, pain, horror, deep sadness, and grief." None of the reasons we find ourselves in hiding are too much or too big for God. He is the God who covers us. He is the God who pursues us. He is the God who seeks those in hiding and says, "I found you, and I see you." **Returning to God is the art of being found by God.** We need to be found by him *again and again*.

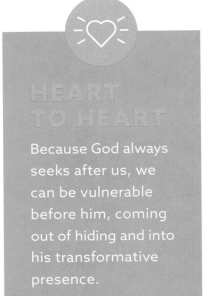

HEART TO HEART

Because God always seeks after us, we can be vulnerable before him, coming out of hiding and into his transformative presence.

WHAT DOES THIS MEAN FOR ME?

Before the fall, being open and vulnerable before God was a good part of being human. Now this sort of openness before God is offered to us again. We can be, as Genesis 2:25 says, naked and unashamed, so to speak, before God and each other. But this requires something to change. This requires that we come out of hiding and allow God's presence to be a sacred, safe space of grace and transformation.

We can compare Adam and Eve's hiding to putting ourselves in a penalty box. We might think, *God isn't ready to see me right now. Not like this.* But that's the voice of shame and lies, the voice of the cunning serpent, Satan. What does God say? "Where are you?" He is looking for us, ready and willing to offer us a covering in the gift of Christ's atoning death.

APPLY THIS: Listen to the song "Lost & Lonely" by Grove Worship. Allow the lyrics to remind you how God comes after you.

18

God
Is Love

IN A FLASH God loves everyone unconditionally; upon receiving his love, we're invited to change and deepen our intimacy.

1 John 4:7-12

Beloved, let us love *one another, for* love *is from God, and whoever* loves *has been born of God and knows God. Anyone who does not love does not know God, because God is* love. *In this the* love of God *was made manifest* among us, that God sent his only

Son into the world, so that we might

love requires a deep level of affection and intimacy

live through him. In this is love,

not that we have loved God but

that he loved us and sent his Son

to be the propitiation for our sins.

Beloved, if God so loved us,

we also ought to love one another.

No one has ever seen God; if we

remains with

love one another, God abides in us

and his love is perfected in us.

Love is a complicated thing. In infancy, we were utterly dependent on having every need provided for us. Studies show anything outside of a loving environment during childhood can result in misunderstanding love well into adulthood.[13] If love wasn't modeled within your childhood environment and you felt overlooked, ignored, or uncared for, it may be hard to express love in a healthy manner as an adult.

The search for love can lead to broken hearts, friend feuds, or fending off bullies. A quest for true love can create an emptiness inside or a desire to be noticed in all the wrong places. We can be left to wonder, *What will fill this pain? What does genuine love even look like?*

FUN FACT

The word *love* in Hebrew and Greek appears 744 times (as a verb and a noun) in most English Bibles.

WHAT HE IS LIKE

Love in the purest form was, is, and will always be found simply in God. God's story is the greatest love story ever told. It's a love story we can't wrap our finite brains around fully. **To define love would be to define God himself.**

God's love is not conditional, based on our performance or status. His love is for all he created. God's love is absolute, complete, stable, unwavering, and continual. His love has no beginning or end and cannot run out, but runs over, touching everything in its path. It's a sustaining, comforting, sacrificial, and fierce love that invites us into intimacy within himself. Although God's love existed before humanity, it is also demonstrated because of humanity. This love is encapsulated within the three persons of the Trinity, which fuses together the bits of humanity that are broken and those who are beautifully restored.

God loves all he created.

(John 3:16–17)

God loves his children.

(1 John 3:1–2)

God *is* love.

(1 John 4:8)

Love was here before the start of time, sustains us through our time here on earth, and extends into eternity. Love is like an active volcano flowing over God's divine attributes, like wisdom, mercy, and peace. Love binds all God's characteristics together (Col. 3:14; 1 Cor. 13) and is a godly virtue that we'll take with us beyond this life (Gal. 5:22–23).

A healthy love doesn't enable bad choices but guides with firm consequences, knowing we were made for more. Think of someone you love deeply. Imagine if they injured your relationship and began pushing you away. What would you do? You would fight for them, offering restoration. God's love is fierce, providing freedom from sin and shame. He is so loving that he sent a solution for the brokenness in humanity: his one and only Son.

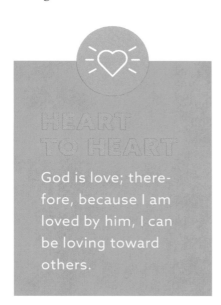

HEART TO HEART

God is love; therefore, because I am loved by him, I can be loving toward others.

In the letter Paul wrote to the Ephesians, he prayed "that you, being rooted and established in love, may have power, together with all the Lord's holy people, to grasp how wide and long and high and deep is the love of Christ, and to know this love that surpasses knowledge—that you may be filled to the measure of all the fullness of God" (3:17–19 NIV). God's love is a healthy love we receive abundantly and seek to model in our lives. God's love is as infinite as his eternal being! Grasping this is part of growing in our faith. As we do, it fuses our broken hearts, fulfills our longing to feel known, and establishes a secure and firm foundation from which we thrive.

LOVE IS AND IS NOT

LOVE	SUPPORTING VERSES	LOVE IS NOT	SUPPORTING VERSES
Is patient	1 Thess. 5:14	Envious	Gal. 5:25–26
Is kind	Eph. 4:32	Boastful	James 4:6
Rejoices with the truth	2 John 1:4	Rude	Phil. 2:3
Bears all things	1 Cor. 9:12	Arrogant	1 Cor. 4:6
Believes all things	Mark 9:23	Insisting on its own way	1 Cor. 10:24
Hopes all things	Rom. 15:13	Irritable	James 1:19–20
Endures all things	Heb. 12:1–3	Resentful	Eph. 4:31
Never ends	Lam. 3:22–23	Rejoicing at wrongdoing	Isa. 5:20

Paul wrote 1 Corinthians 13:4–8, a familiar passage often quoted at weddings. We've converted these verses into a chart showing what love is and is not. **When you encounter God's love, you're empowered to give his love as you align your actions under the authority of Scripture.**

WHAT DOES THIS MEAN FOR ME?

When I (Jenny) think of God's love, I often recall the experiences God and I have shared. God sustained me with peace during an illness, provided for me after my family and I lost three-quarters of our income during the COVID crisis, and repeatedly reminded me he is with me. Even this response to his love reveals selfish motives. I listed out reasons why I love God based on all the things he does for me.

If God was all you ever had and nothing more, would that satisfy your longing for connection and care? We pray for all of us that it does. May we remember that we don't worship him because of his blessings. Jesus doesn't owe us anything. His love is more than enough.

The love we desire may come from a sinful longing for satisfaction, or thinking we have to do something to get it. The love we give may become weary, depleted, or have ulterior motives. The way we experience true love will be perfected in eternity, but in the waiting, we're equipped by God's love to do the fighting and pursue him, the very embodiment of love itself. **When we want to see love in action, look at Jesus.** The Gospels show us what love on the move looks like.

Love really is the gift that keeps on giving. It's a fruit of the Spirit that we'll continue to develop as we learn how to give love (Gal. 5:22–23). But first, we must understand how to receive God's love. We're undeserving of his love, yet he freely gives it! So as God prompts us to do the impossible, we love our enemies (Matt. 5:44) and our neighbors just like we love ourselves (Matt. 22:39–40). We must abide in God, as he in us (John 15:1–17).

APPLY THIS: Think of a neighbor or someone you'd consider an enemy. Now prayerfully consider one way to demonstrate God's love to that person. Following the "love is" side of our chart, go and put love into action without expecting anything in return.

19

God Is Creative

 IN A FLASH The triune God is the ultimate Creator, bringing order and beauty out of chaos and brokenness.

Revelation 4:11

Worthy are you, our Lord and God, to receive glory and honor and power, for you created all *things, and by* your will *they existed and were* created.

Psalm 33:9–11

The darkness gets a bad rap. We get it; mystery often lurks behind the black curtain of gloom. The unknown can be scary, a place for fear to reside. We might wonder, *Is that really a pile of clothes in my bedroom, or am I about to get murdered?* Maybe that's where the old saying "Nothing good ever happens after midnight" came from.

But what if we flipped the script? **Imagine the unknown as a place of unlimited potential, like a theater show, dimming the lights into the darkness to communicate that something majestic is about to unfold.** As you lay your head on your pillow at night, close your eyes, tune out the distractions, and invite yourself to rest, remember that the sun always rises out of the darkness, bringing a new day. What if the place void of light isn't something to fear but a place where our creative God breaks through to establish something new?

WHAT HE IS LIKE

Darkness is often a metaphor for spiritual blindness, sin, eternal death, the enemy, or Satan. The thing we often forget about darkness is that it existed before creation, and terror and torment did not reside there. God was there before evil claimed the shadows as its own. **God was in the darkness, chaos, and formlessness. What if he created these things to establish a desperation for light, order, and meaning?** It reminds us of Psalm 139:11–12: "If I say, 'Surely the darkness will hide me, and the light around me will be night'—even the darkness is not dark to you. The night shines like the day; darkness and light are alike to you" (CSB). As we read about good and evil in the Bible, do you know what always happens? The light permeates the darkness (see, for example, John 1:5).

As we continue to understand different theological truths, understanding and embracing God as the ultimate Creator is key! Because if we don't look for his creativity, we'll miss the wonder, awe, and beauty that shape us. God is a master painter who sees the empty canvas and brings it to life.

In Genesis 1, God saw potential in the void, darkness, and nothingness. To him, it was a canvas worth painting. As he spoke, things were set into motion as the world was formed and filled. The dark was fused with light, creating a rhythm to the day; heaven and earth

GOD CREATED

> In the beginning, God created the heavens and the earth. The earth was without form and void, and darkness was over the face of the deep. And the Spirit of God was hovering over the face of the waters. And God said, "Let there be light." (Gen. 1:1–3)

> I form light and create darkness; I make well-being and create calamity; I am the LORD, who does all these things. (Isa. 45:7)

> By faith we understand that the universe was created by the word of God, so that what is seen was not made out of things that are visible. (Heb. 11:3)

> For God, who said, "Let light shine out of darkness," has shone in our hearts to give the light of the knowledge of the glory of God in the face of Jesus Christ. (2 Cor. 4:6)

were formed; creation, plants, and people were built with purpose through those holy-infused brushstrokes. What was once empty was filled by the ultimate Creator. Genesis 1 shows God actively bringing things into existence and putting creation in order. Holy Spirit hovered over the face of the waters (v. 2), and with God's spoken word, the canvas was filled with beauty, splendor, and captivating things. Seven different times God called his creation good.

Our Creator God didn't stop after forming the earth. He continues to spark a world of wonder! There's a need for creative expression, as people take ownership within the world in their careers and callings and as the gospel spreads to the ends of the earth. In the Bible, David was a songwriter and worshipper (1 Chron. 16), Bezalel was the chief artisan who built the tabernacle with divine guidance (Ex. 31:1–6), and Jesus's earthly job was carpenter (Mark 6:3).

Our salvation experience directly parallels God's creative expression in crafting night and day. John 8:12 says, "Again Jesus spoke to them, saying, 'I am the light of the world. Whoever follows me will not walk in darkness, but will have the light of life.'" It's fascinating to think how the light (Jesus) illuminates our soul in the darkness. Second Corinthians 4:6 says, "For God, who said, 'Let light shine out of darkness,' has shone in our hearts to

FUN FACT

Creation itself is waiting to be resurrected along with the redeemed believers (Rom. 8:18–25), so even the most beautiful places on earth are still broken and awaiting their redemption.

give the light of the knowledge of the glory of God in the face of Jesus Christ." The sin and terror of death do not stay hidden in the shadows but are obliterated by a creative God.

We don't always see the full picture of what God creates in the darkness or within the brokenness, but we encounter hope as we get to know his character better. Sometimes he works through a person to provide a creative solution to a social-justice problem, crafts a supernatural miracle to a weary body, or inspires and develops the unique talents of his people! God's creativity is beautiful, unrivaled, and unlimited. When we catch a glimpse of his creative expression, it's a piece of heaven invading earth. Revelation 21:5 says that God will make "all things new" when he forms a new heaven and earth. His creativity will bring an end to chaos and destruction! The new creation is our ultimate hope, and God's creativity, without the marring effects of sin, will be on full display.

HEART TO HEART

God's creativity inspires us to reflect care and innovation into the world.

WHAT DOES THIS MEAN FOR ME?

God's creative nature didn't stop at creation; it extended to you (and beyond). You are not the result of some random, chaotic chemical accident; you are crafted with thought, dignity, and purpose. Most importantly, you were created for him! "For we are his workmanship, created in Christ Jesus for good works, which God prepared beforehand, that we should walk in them" (Eph. 2:10). The very one who created us invites us, image-bearing believers, to join in his creative work—all for his glory and the good of others.

True creativity is expressed when partnered with the ultimate Creator. From this place, our creativity shines into the darkness. Embrace the creativity that is before you! Yes, your creativity may move beyond art or music, as it often expands beyond words and into solutions, numbers, and different forms of expression. As you embrace God's creativity for yourself, you flow within the very nature of who he is. This is an act of worship. Whether creating for fun, just because, with your kids, for a career, or through professional projects, making space to create leaves a mark on the world.

Christians should be the innovators, problem solvers, teachers, coaches, scientists, fashion designers, entertainers, and creators infused with the creative DNA of our maker. You are created to create! No matter what profession, hobby, or calling we have—creativity is part of who we are as God's image bearers. As you walk into areas of influence for God, hope prevails. We're not asking you to create "Christian art" (unless you want to); we're asking you to create whatever he puts on your heart. God can use this divinely inspired stuff to spark a light of hope and healing over anyone who connects with it. Let's be the most dazzling creators out there, as we connect humanity with the Light of the World!

APPLY THIS: Healthy creative expression can be an act of worship! What were a few creative things you loved to do as a child? Rekindle that spark, and go and create in that same way today. If you want to learn more about God-given creativity, check out *Courageous Creative* by Jenny Randle.

20

God Gives Grace

IN A FLASH Grace is God's radical gift of redemption.

Ephesians 2:1-10

past tense, Col. 2:13

And you *were dead* in the *trespasses*

.... moral failure

and *sins* in which you once walked,

.... wrongdoing toward God

following the course of this world,

following the prince of the power

Satan ....

of the air, the *spirit* that is now at

work in the sons of disobedience—

.... Unbeliever

among whom we all once lived

in the passions of our flesh, carrying

out the desires of the body and the mind, and were by nature children of wrath, like the rest of mankind. But God, being rich in mercy, because of the great love with which he loved us, even when we were dead in our trespasses, made us alive together with Christ—by grace you have been saved—and raised us up with him and seated us with him in the heavenly places in Christ Jesus, so that in the coming ages he might show the immeasurable riches of his grace in kindness toward us in Christ Jesus. For by grace you have been

1 Pet. 1:5

saved through faith. And this is not

2 Cor. 3:5

your own doing; it is the gift of God, not a result of works, so that no one may boast. For we are his workmanship, created in Christ Jesus for good works, which God prepared beforehand, that we should walk in them.

Parenting is hard. I (Jenny) remember the time my preschool-aged child sat in the corner in a time-out. Typical kid stuff put them there, probably climbing onto the dining room table again, yelling, "Nobody eats pizza," while in fact, eating (and throwing) pizza. As I began the timer for three minutes, trying not to laugh, I prompted my child to take some time to process the situation that unfolded. This little adorable human spoke up from the chair-of-chill and asked, "Mama, will you extend grace to me and bust me out of here?"

Parents often enjoy teaching our children the principle of grace by demonstrating it within our relationship. We want them to know that they can't earn grace, perform for it, or muster enough prayers to receive it. It is just freely given by a God who loves us so much he wants us free.

So in moments when our kids were reaping the consequences of poor actions, we'd extend favor toward them by hugging it out and dramatically gazing into their eyes and saying, "I love you so much that I'm extending grace to you right now. Just like God does for us." Then they'd be delivered from that time-out chair early, rather than getting the consequence they deserved. It's a beautiful illustration of how God's love and kindness sets us free, even when we don't deserve it.

At first, when my children encountered this gift of grace, their eyes grew big, and the very concept astounded them. But in this pizza-throwing moment, the tables turned, and I saw a glimpse of an unhealthy pattern forming. With every act of disobedience or defiance, the question of grace was uttered before their butt even landed in that time-out chair. Perhaps they thought this gift of forgiveness was a free pass to create mass chaos. So in understanding God's beautiful gift of grace, the questions we pose today are, how does God's grace impact us, and do we have any responsibility in it?

WHAT HE IS LIKE

In Ephesians 2:1–10, the apostle Paul painted a stark comparison between what humans are by nature (vv. 1–3) and what they can become because of God and his grace (vv. 4–10). We call this the *grace erase*. It's a space where the human condition is saturated and overpowered by divine compassion, where the brutality of the world is erased by God's grace and goodness.

God's favor toward us is unmerited, undeserved, and freely given. God is good, and this goodness has no correlation to what fallen humanity does or does not do. A loving God manifests his grace, saving our broken souls, and produces a beautiful faith in Christ. Grace is given, whether or not it is accepted. Through the power of Holy Spirit, by faith, we walk through the door entering God's kingdom. **Christ is the key to our salvation, and grace is the hand that turns the key, unlocking a relationship with our Creator.** We, however, are called to move our feet. And as we do, God gifts measures of grace and favor, equipping us in the areas where his will leads us.

GIFT OF GRACE

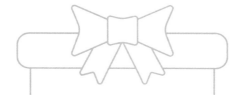

UNBELIEVER

Dead
Sinner
Child of wrath

Follower of the world

Led with the passion
of the flesh
Created for redemption

BUT GOD...
Led by love and mercy,
by grace God saves
through faith in
Christ alone

BELIEVER

Made alive with Christ
Saint
Child of God

Follower of his Word

Led with a passion by
Holy Spirit
Created for good works

God's great love saves, and he
continues to show his kindness and favor
to his followers through relationship.

WHAT DOES THIS MEAN FOR ME?

We once walked in sin and wrongdoings toward God, and now we walk in the path of sainthood, unpacking the good things God has for us. **This gift of grace is free, but how we steward it is our responsibility. We can trash it, honor it, or regift it altogether.**

So just as a child in the face of dire consequences receives a free gift of grace, we shouldn't squander what we've been given by committing the same mistakes repeatedly. Your life can be an all-encompassing thank-you to what God has given you. His loving grace isn't a reason for bargaining, boasting, or even doing your own thing. It's a place of receiving and being redeemed, a place of regifting the love and grace that are freely given. Just as the author in Hebrews wrote, "Let us then with confidence draw near to the throne of grace, that we may receive mercy and find grace to help in time of need" (Heb. 4:16). Take hold of God's gift, and unlock all the goodness that comes from his grace!

HEART TO HEART

God is the greatest gift-giver; because he has given us his favor, we can give favor to those who need to be lifted up.

APPLY THIS: Study Ephesians 1:3–14. Journal through all the ways you see God's gift of grace on display.

21

God Is Rich

IN A FLASH God gives generously out of his abundance.

1 Timothy 6:17-19

As for the `rich` in this present age,
.... Titus 2:12

charge them not to be haughty,

nor to set their hopes on the

uncertainty of `riches,` but on God,

who `richly` provides us with

everything to enjoy. They are to do

good, to be `rich` in good works,

to be generous and ready to share,

thus storing up treasure for

Matt. 6:19–20 says do not store up earthly treasures but treasures in heaven

themselves as a good foundation for

the future, so that they may

take hold of that which is truly life.

1 Tim. 6:12 shares we must take hold of eternal life

The prosperity gospel. A phrase used in Christianity to describe a certain theology (we call it *fakeology)* of beliefs surrounding success, health, and financial provision. To put it bluntly, the belief is that Christians have an all-access pass to health, wealth, and prosperity. Prosperity preachers urge people to enlist Christ to enrich their lives, creating a transactional relationship. Now depending on your theological bias, you may have just cringed a little or started a slow clap, throwing bazillions in the air. If you're over there throwing the money, give us some, because we're about to throw some shade on that prosperity-gospel game.

God cares about finances, but not in the way you may think. He cares that your finances don't *own* you, cause greed, or distort your priorities. Money *isn't* evil, but loving money *is* (1 Tim. 6:10). Meanwhile, the root of all kinds of good things is *God.* So when we talk about God being rich, we are emphasizing something different than the American Dream.

WHAT HE IS LIKE

Every attribute of God (his love, grace, and so on) is rich in a different way than we might think. We generally talk about wealth in quantifiable terms, but since God is infinite, his abundance cannot be quantified. For example, his grace is beyond measure, literally! "Every good gift and every perfect gift is from above, coming down from the Father of lights" (James 1:17). Our triune God is good and munificent (generous), giving the most magnificent gift: himself. Ephesians 3:8 says there are unsearchable riches of Christ. Our human brains don't have the capacity to even understand the depth of abundance we have because of Jesus. And this abundance isn't gained in the natural, but the supernatural.

Those who follow Christ need to care less about monetary riches and more about spiritual riches. What if we didn't obsess over the contents of our bank accounts and instead focused on the contents of our hearts? There's fruit that flows from following Christ. God manifests his power, grace, and might throughout our lives.

You can have bazillions of dollars or barely anything, yet God can be empowering you to use your wealth (or lack of) honorably and for his good. He gives grace and wisdom generously to guide our lives on a path toward him. His riches go beyond money and worldly versions of success. He is rich in mercy, love, grace, kindness, might—all the character traits we've been studying throughout *Flash Theology*. God is abundant in both resources and supernatural riches.

VERSES TO REFLECT ON

Do you presume on the **riches of his kindness** and forbearance and patience, not knowing that God's kindness is meant to lead you to repentance? (Rom. 2:4)

For there is no distinction between Jew and Greek; for the same Lord is Lord of all, bestowing his **riches** on all who call on him. (Rom. 10:12)

Oh, the depth of the **riches** and wisdom and knowledge of God! How unsearchable are his judgments and how inscrutable his ways! (Rom. 11:33)

In him we have redemption through his blood, the forgiveness of our trespasses, according to the **riches** of his grace, which he lavished upon us, in all wisdom and insight making known to us the mystery of his will, according to his purpose, which he set forth in Christ. (Eph. 1:7–9)

But God, being **rich in mercy,** because of the great love with which he loved us, even when we were dead in our trespasses, made us alive together with Christ—by grace you have been saved—and raised us up with him and seated us with him in the heavenly places in Christ Jesus. (Eph. 2:4–6)

HEART TO HEART

We live out of God's abundance and are inspired to generosity.

WHAT DOES THIS MEAN FOR ME?

As a little girl, I (Jenny) remember a time my dad took my brother and me out for fast food. As we were digging through our food, my dad asked for some french fries. I began to aggressively shove my fries in my face, ignoring the question altogether, but not my younger brother. He responded with maturity beyond his years. My preschool-aged brother, knowing who had provided the fries, said, "They're not mine anyway," and gave them to his father. In a similar way, since Christ paid the price, we can only give back what is already his. Just as we noted above, in 1 Timothy 6:17, we must be rich in God and good stewards of all he's given.

It reminds us of this saying in the marketing world: "There's riches in the niches." The saying means that the more you focus on the place you fit, the more abundance follows. What if we implement that same idea, yet the riches are spiritual and our niche is our relationship with God? So instead of desiring, wanting, or needing fame and fortune, we focus our thoughts on God and how he desires us to be rich in grace, faith, love, and more. We shift our focus from us to God and his generous character. As Christ followers, our riches aren't found in hundred-dollar bills, but in intimacy with God himself. We then begin to reflect what we behold.

In the Bible, we see patterns of people demonstrating godly character by living generously. Leviticus 27:30 indicates that tithing (giving 10 percent) was central to God's law. The Israelites didn't wait to feel inspired to give; it was just something they did. In the New Testament, as the early church was getting started, Christ followers strengthened the church by living generously, offering hospitality, and supporting the work of the ministry. **We don't need to ask God if we should be generous; we just need to show up and do it.**

APPLY THIS: Demonstrate generosity today or this weekend. Better your community or support the mission of your church by giving money or volunteering your time and talents wherever needed.

22

God Is Merciful

 IN A FLASH God is eager to show us mercy, canceling our debts and making a way for new beginnings.

Micah 7:18-19

Micah's name means "who is like the Lord?"

Who is a God like you,

pardoning iniquity and passing

over transgression for the

remnant of his inheritance?

He does not retain his anger

forever, because he delights in

It makes God happy to act with love.

steadfast love. He will again

have compassion on us; he will

·············· Like a military leader trampling over enemies, so God subdues our iniquities.

tread our iniquities underfoot.

You will cast all our sins into

Every single one: past, present, and future ··············

the depths of the sea.

In the first movie of Christopher Nolan's famous Dark Knight trilogy, *Batman Begins*, Bruce Wayne completes his apprenticeship to the League of Shadows and has to prove his loyalty or, in the words of Ra's al Ghul, his "commitment to justice." So the League brings a murderer and gives Bruce a sword. He has been training for years to fight criminals, and here is his chance to be one's executioner. Bruce explains that, as passionate as he is about fighting injustice, he does not intend on becoming an executioner. Ra's al Ghul challenges Bruce's position, saying, "Your compassion is a weakness your enemies will not share." Bruce replies, "That's why it's so important. It separates us from them." His response transcends the film and should reflect a Christian's heart. It does, indeed, reflect God's heart.

WHAT HE IS LIKE

Jonah is one of the oddest prophets in the Bible for three reasons. He reluctantly shared God's Word. He was the only prophet whose message was heeded by his audience! And he was successful in bringing the Ninevites to repentance, despite hoping they would be obliterated by God. Not to mention, he got thrown into the ocean, swallowed by a fish, and lived to tell the tale!

Before we judge Jonah too harshly, let's give him some slack. Was he wrong in his actions? Absolutely! But context helps explain his motivations. Nineveh was the capital of Assyria, the world superpower that threatened the safety and well-being of Israel. On top of that, they were the most pagan of pagans. They worshipped false gods and were known for their brutality toward conquered peoples, especially for how they mistreated women. They epitomized sin and evil. *You and I would probably hate Nineveh too.*

But instead of wiping Nineveh from the face of the earth, God felt compassion for them: "And should not I pity Nineveh, that great city, in which there are more than 120,000 persons who do not know their right hand from their left, and also much cattle?" (Jon. 4:11).

Make no mistake, God knew the injustice the Ninevites had perpetrated. In fact, Jonah was originally commissioned to proclaim that God had lost patience with their wickedness (1:2). God is not apathetic about the atrocities caused by sinful people, but he prefers to triumph over evil by converting sinners rather than crushing them. Perhaps this is what James, the earthly brother of Jesus, meant when he wrote to believers, "Mercy triumphs over judgment" (James 2:13). **It's not that God makes light of our sin; he just makes more of his mercy. God is far more willing to give mercy than humans are willing to ask for it.**

God's merciful heart is what caused Jonah to pray, "O LORD, is not this what I said when I was yet in my country? That is why I made haste to flee to Tarshish; for I knew that you are a gracious God and _merciful_, slow to anger and abounding in steadfast love, and relenting from disaster" (Jon. 4:2). Jonah's declaration of God's character is almost identical in wording to other places in the Old Testament (Ex. 34:6; Ps. 103:8; 145:8; Joel

SUMMARIZING THE STORY OF JONAH

GOD'S WORD	JONAH'S RESPONSE	GOD'S ACTION	OUTCOME
God called Jonah to go to Nineveh and confront their evil (1:2).	Jonah fled the far opposite direction, hoping to evade the task, because he hated the Ninevites (1:3).	God caused a great storm to prevent the boat Jonah was on from getting to Tarshish (1:4–6).	Jonah was thrown into the sea, the storm stopped, and the pagan sailors feared the Lord (1:7–16).
God rescued Jonah and spoke to him to go to Nineveh with his message (3:1–2).	Jonah only went to part of Nineveh and told them half of the message (3:3–4).	God moved in the people's hearts despite Jonah's half-hearted preaching (3:5–9).	The king led the people to repent, and God relented from destroying Nineveh (3:10), which infuriated Jonah (4:1–3).
God confronted Jonah's unmerciful heart and revealed his compassion on the evil people of Nineveh (4:9–11).	Unknown, because the book ends with God's word to Jonah (4:11).	God used the plant and its shade to show Jonah his selfish and misled heart (4:5–11).	Readers are left to think about how we might respond to God's generous mercy and compassion toward our own enemies.

2:13). Jonah had sound theology, but the God-truths never became heart-realities for him. It is a tragedy when our knowledge is divorced from our hearts.

FUN FACT

Jonah 4:2 is the only time in the Old Testament where God's mercy is the cause for criticism instead of praise. In the New Testament, Jesus was often criticized for his mercy. For example, in Matthew 9:9–12, Jesus called Matthew (a tax collector) to be one of his disciples. This caused uproar among the Pharisees, but Jesus explained that he came like a physician for the sick and that he desired people to learn what mercy was.

HEART TO HEART

The more we experience God's mercy, the more we are to exemplify mercy toward others.

WHAT DOES THIS MEAN FOR ME?

Mercy is considered a hallmark of the Father's heart (Luke 6:36). Exemplifying God's mercy often requires we dive deeper into his mercy so that we see just how deep it is! Follow us on this wordplay here.

One of the best, most illustrative passages of Scripture regarding God's mercy is found in Micah 7:18–19. Note the end of verse 19: "You will cast all our sins into the depths of the sea."

For the ancient Israelites, the *bottom* of the ocean was Sheol, the realm of the dead.[14] So for God to throw their sins into the depths of the ocean was to send them to Sheol—to "kill" the very sins that formerly had killed them. What a satisfying reversal! The mercy God offers to you in Christ takes your track record of sin (past, present, and future) and buries it in the deepest part of the sea—where dead things go *and don't come back!*

One way that our God is not like any other so-called god (Mic. 7:18) is because of his generous mercy. In fact, Scripture says that God is "rich in mercy" (Eph. 2:4). So next time you think you are exhausting the mercy of God, just remember that he has an abounding and rich supply of it! Charles Spurgeon reminds us: "God's mercy is so great, that you may sooner drain the sea of its water, or deprive the sun of his light, or make space too narrow, than diminish the great mercy of God."[15]

Let's think more about that for a second. Imagine you have a red plastic cup in your hand and you go to the beach to gaze at the ocean. Then picture dipping the cup into the ocean and filling it with water for every single sin you have ever committed—and add a couple hundred thousand extra scoops for all the sins you have committed without acknowledging! You could keep dipping that red plastic cup into the water until you passed out, or until you died from old age—and you know what? *You still wouldn't get even close* to emptying the ocean of water. **You would sooner drain the ocean of water than you would exhaust God of his mercy.**

God's mercy offers us a new beginning. The question is: What will *you* do with it?

APPLY THIS: Schedule a time to go to a large body of water like an ocean, lake, or heck, run the water in your bathtub if you need to. Bring an empty cup with you. And while having a genuine moment of solitude, take time to repent, then rest in and receive God's mercy as you continually fill up the cup and pour out the water—reminding yourself of God's bottomless, never-ending mercy toward you.

23

God Is Just

IN A FLASH God's justice is an expression of his love as he intervenes to put an end to evil.

Psalm 96:9-13 (NLT)

*Worship the L*ORD *in all his holy splendor. Let all the earth tremble before him. Tell all the nations, "The L*ORD reigns!" *The world*

This is the verbal form of the Hebrew word for "king."

stands firm and cannot be shaken.

He will judge all peoples fairly.

Let the heavens be glad, and the

earth rejoice! Let the sea and everything in it shout his praise! Let the fields and their crops burst out with joy! Let the trees of the forest sing for joy before the LORD, for he is coming!

God's coming judgment is the reason for creation's celebration.

He is coming to judge the earth. He will judge the world with justice, and the nations with his truth.

WHAT HE IS LIKE

It is fitting to talk about God's justice immediately after talking about his mercy. God's preference is to lead with mercy, and he certainly desires to act with mercy toward his creation. However, God is good and just, so he knows when to say, "Enough is enough." God's justice stems from his love. His love is fierce, so he defends his creation against those who devote themselves to evil and oppression. **A God who is indifferent toward evil is not worthy of our worship.**

We've already seen God's mercy on display in the story of Jonah and Nineveh. Want to know a great place to see God's justice? Check out the little book of Nahum. Nahum's prophecy of judgment is directed toward Nineveh, proclaiming the coming end of their kingdom, a judgment that would be certain and irrevocable.

The vast Assyrian Empire was established by bloodshed and massacre, cruelty and torture, destruction, plundering, and exiling, such as has seldom been seen in history. Yet, astoundingly, there was a generation of Ninevites who had turned the tide, owned their sin against God, and repented (Jon. 4). A little more than a century later, though—and we don't have to be experts in history to know that a lot can happen in one hundred years—the Ninevites had returned to their wicked ways.

God does not ignore the cries of people suffering under the cruelty of evil rulers. (And let's remember, God waited a hundred years before signaling Nineveh's downfall.) The fall of Nineveh acts as an example for how all other rebellious nations will be dealt with on God's timing. God won't allow evil and injustice to endure.

God is the righteous judge who will intervene and end evil in due time. When you feel tired of seeing the bad guys getting away with what they do, rest assured that evil does not go unnoticed on God's watch. Nahum shows us that when God wants to end evil, he gives it a fatal wound (Nah. 3:18–19). While the Old Testament has sections of judgment on specific geographical parts of the world, the New Testament speaks of God's justice having a decisive and all-encompassing reach at the return of the Lord Jesus.

GOD'S DECISIVE JUDGMENT ON NINEVEH IN NAHUM

VERSE	REFERENCE
The LORD is good, a refuge in times of trouble. He cares for those who trust in him, but with an overwhelming flood he will make an end of Nineveh; he will pursue his foes into the realm of darkness.	Nah. 1:7–8 (NIV)
The LORD has given a command concerning you, Nineveh: "You will have no descendants to bear your name. I will destroy the images and idols that are in the temple of your gods. I will prepare your grave, for you are vile."	Nah. 1:14 (NIV)
"I am against you," declares the LORD Almighty. "I will burn up your chariots in smoke, and the sword will devour your young lions. I will leave you no prey on the earth. The voices of your messengers will no longer be heard."	Nah. 2:13 (NIV)
Nothing can heal you; your wound is fatal. All who hear the news about you clap their hands at your fall, for who has not felt your endless cruelty?	Nah. 3:19 (NIV)

Read Psalms 96, 97, and 98 (especially 96:7–13), and you will see that all creation—including trees, mountains, and rivers—is depicted as celebrating God's coming judgment! When God comes to judge the world, he will right the wrongs, overthrow the oppressors, tear down the tyrants, vindicate the vulnerable, and restore his righteous rule over all the world. **God's just judgment isn't contradictory to the gospel; it is part of what makes the gospel *good news*!**

FUN FACT

Nahum's name means "comforted," which is no coincidence for the name of the book. God is also seen as the comforter who defends the disenfranchised. He comforted Judah with this message of salvation through the judgment of the cruel Assyrians.

Judging from Nahum, it is best to understand God's justice as *delayed*, not *denied*. God's justice is delayed in that he gives individuals time to respond to his mercy, change their hearts and ways, and draw near to him. However, God's justice will never be denied. Evil will be eradicated forever. The "fatal wound" of Nineveh is a foreshadowing of the fatal wound that has been given to the domain of darkness. Because of Jesus's death and resurrection, sin and death have received their death blow and are bleeding out. The Lord will have the final word. God's delay is a time of mercy for sinners to come to repentance. God's yearning is salvation for any and all (2 Pet. 3:9). However, heed the words of the prophet: the Lord is coming to judge the world because of sin and evil.

N. T. Wright reconciled God's love and justice with eloquence: "God is the living and loving creator, who must either judge the world or stand accused of injustice, of letting wickedness triumph. People who have lived in societies where evil flourishes unchecked will tell you that it is a nightmare. To live in a world where that was the case for ever would be hell."[16]

Proverbs 21:15 says, "Justice is a joy to the godly, but it terrifies evildoers" (NLT). Evil trembles, because its time is ticking away. We know where God stands. Where do we stand? If we stand with him, we can—like all creation—rejoice that he is coming to set all things right and make all things new.

WHAT DOES THIS MEAN FOR ME?

In his Sermon on the Mount, Jesus said, "Blessed are those who hunger and thirst for righteousness, for they shall be satisfied" (Matt. 5:6). The word translated "righteousness" comes from the Greek word *dikaiosynē*, which means both "righteousness" and "justice." They are the same word in both Greek and Hebrew, so you can't talk about one without the other. Recall the last time you felt so thirsty that all you could think about was finding water to drink. What if we had the same determination to see God's righteousness and justice prevail?

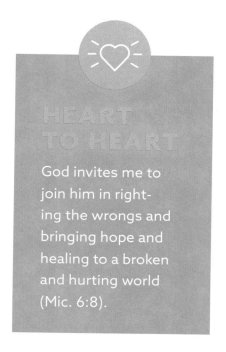

HEART TO HEART

God invites me to join him in righting the wrongs and bringing hope and healing to a broken and hurting world (Mic. 6:8).

Now before we raise up arms or become keyboard warriors on social media platforms, we're not to fight for justice the way we see modeled in our world or history itself. Jesus is our example. As you read the Gospels, take note of what Jesus did when he encountered a wrong and how he made it right. And while you and I are not God incarnate, God *has* equipped us, the Church, with talents, gifts, and resources to meet the needs we see. But justice will likely cost us. Sacrifice—Christ on the cross—was what it took to secure our ultimate justice; why would we expect it to be easy?

In 2021, the church where I (Brayden) am currently on staff helped reach a monumental goal. For the first time ever, the country of Liberia—*every single tribe and person*—has sustainable access to clean drinking water. This came about through a multi-year, multi-church partnership with two nonprofits and the above and beyond generosity of many Christians. Water was the tool, and the gospel was the goal. The locals were so excited about what was happening that they would announce the coming of clean water to the next tribe, shouting: "Clean water is coming! Jesus is bringing it!" This is just one incredible way in which we see God's justice prevail, where people's needs are met through clean water as they are also introduced to the living water that Jesus provides (John 4:14; 7:38).

And beyond any resource we have, God has given us his empowering presence through Holy Spirit. Let's be honest: we wildly underestimate what he might do through us. But what would happen if our church communities found their voice and acted against evil and injustice?

APPLY THIS: Make a list of your God-given convictions or responses you have toward something that needs restoration. Prayerfully ask God how you or your church can take practical steps to bring resolution to the problem.

24

God Listens

IN A FLASH God's ear is tuned in to those who follow him.

1 John 5:13-14

I write these things to you

·········· the apostle John

who believe in the name of the Son

of God, that you may know that

you have eternal life. And this is the

confidence *that we have toward*

1 John 2:28 ··········   ·········· 1 John 3:22

him, that if we ask anything

according to his will he hears us.

God's desired purpose ··········

When you think of being a good listener, you usually picture a person giving their undivided attention, nodding at the right moments, and repeating what was said. Have you ever felt truly seen and heard? What was it like? For some, it's when you can't quite gather your thoughts, but the person listening communicates back to you what you wanted to say, or when they ask the question that cuts to the heart of the matter. Maybe it was the time the person listening saw through your fake smile and leaned in a little more to show that you're not alone.

Being a good listener is more than just actively taking notice of what one is hearing. A *Harvard Business Review* study said that "people perceive the best listeners to be those who periodically ask questions that promote discovery and insight. These questions gently challenge old assumptions, but do so in a constructive way."[17] Feeling listened to is more than just being heard; it's being seen too.

WHAT HE IS LIKE

During Jesus's public ministry, he listened, observed, and led people into significant transformation and growth. He sat with people and really paid attention (see, for example, Matt. 9:9–13). He engaged with people from all walks of life without bias or prejudice. God not only listened to the lost and those he loved but also pointed them to hope in the process. The response he offered was himself.

God was both present and powerful. In fact, the early church grew after Jesus's death and resurrection, as Holy Spirit empowered Christ followers to break down cultural and societal norms (see, for example, Acts 10–11). The apostles were present with people, listening to their stories and learning who they were. Holy Spirit empowered them to preach the good news in light of what they'd heard. Holy Spirit helps us listen by producing patience, love, kindness, gentleness, and so much more (Gal. 5:22–23).

The Lord modeled listening and leaned into questions. His listening offered safety and security. Jesus did this because he cared about people and what they had to say, while also understanding the bigger picture of accomplishing the redemption of humanity. This care and compassion were why he often took the time to respond with questions. In probing a little deeper, he revealed the true desires of a person's heart. **God listens and responds in a way that empowers others to become both self-aware and God-aware.**

Listening is easy; learning to process what you've heard is hard. God, being God, has divine wisdom to read between the lines. In Exodus 3, at the burning bush, God called Moses to take the lead in liberating the Israelites from Egypt. How did Moses respond to this great call? Moses told God all the reasons why he was unavailable, unable, and unqualified. God listened to each excuse and simply pointed Moses back to himself. When Moses tried to put the weight of the world on his own shoulders, God reminded him who he is: the great I AM (Ex. 3:11–15). This is what it looks like to have a relationship with a divine and holy God. **In his listening, God reads between the lines of your discomfort, distrust, doubt, or discouragement, and he finds a way to remind you about himself.** He is the one who delivers you, dwells with and in you, and invites you to dream with him!

GOD LISTENS

STYLE OF LISTENING	EXAMPLE PASSAGE
Rapport listening Communicates with all types of people with the intention of strengthening relationship	Luke 7:36–50
Critical listening Connects with follow-up questions and evaluates the truth in what is being heard	Luke 10:23–28
Sympathetic listening Considers all the conditions beyond what is seen and "hears" emotions and feelings	Luke 20:19–26

HEART TO HEART

As we pray, God listens to our voice and leads us where to go.

WHAT DOES THIS MEAN FOR ME?

God listens. He hears and knows everything. However, there is something unique in how he listens to his children, who are in a relationship with the triune God. We have a friend and Father in him; there's relational equity. Similar to how a parent would respond to their child versus a stranger, God's love is attentive and absolute. We can be 100 percent secure in knowing that God attends to us as we seek him in both worry and worship. Listening strengthens relationships—and it should go both ways.

VERSES TO REFLECT ON

I waited patiently for the LORD;
he inclined to me and heard my cry.
(Ps. 40:1)

When the righteous cry for help, the LORD hears and delivers them out of all their troubles. (Ps. 34:17)

And this is the confidence that we have toward him, that if we ask anything according to his will he hears us. And if we know that he hears us in whatever we ask, we know that we have the requests that we have asked of him. (1 John 5:14–15)

Prayer is a two-way dialogue. In Matthew 6:7, Jesus warned, "When you pray, don't babble like the Gentiles, since they imagine they'll be heard for their many words" (CSB). The Greco-Roman pagan religions taught that you could pester the gods so much they would give you what you wanted. And if one god wouldn't listen, you could always try a different one. After all, there were dozens of gods in the Greco-Roman pantheon. The problem was that they didn't really care—well, and also, they were false gods.

The pagan belief was that their gods would answer your prayer only if you entertained them enough or could do something in return for them. That isn't love—it's a transactional relationship where neither person actually cares about the other, except what they can get from each other. Babbling, pestering, and performing is not the way to pray, and as Christians, if we do, we're practicing false religion.

God looks at the heart. He is not impressed by prayers of showmanship or attempts to manipulate him through technique or babbling on. God is not your genie; he is your Father. A genie gives you what you want with no care or concern for how it affects you. A good father gives you what you need because he cares about how it affects you.

If we believe Scripture and know that God knows what we need before we even ask (Matt. 6:8), then why do we pray? Unlike the pagan gods of the Greco-Roman world, God is never too busy to listen and tend to our prayers. He is a caring Father who anticipates our needs before we even ask. We pray because prayer is more about intimate companionship versus informational communication. It's a two-way dialogue.

If we ask anything according to his will, he hears us (1 John 5:14). That doesn't mean he always responds the way we desire. Since his way is always the best way, we should seek to understand and pray his promises rather than our own shortsighted desires!

Most people don't have a problem talking to God, but many of us have a problem listening to him. During prayer, we often fill our spaces of solitude with safety nets of security—security found in social media alerts, that call from our bestie, or even our latest and greatest Christian devotional. These things and more can serve as distractions from hearing God respond to our pleas, praise, or even the petitioning of his promises. In the listening, through the stillness, though, we learn the will of our Father. Just as God listens to us, may we lean in and listen to him!

APPLY THIS: Spend at least twenty minutes in silence. Learn to be still and listen to God. Does he ask a question of you, offer compassion through supernatural peace, or reveal something deeper hidden underneath the surface?

25

God Is a Promise Keeper

IN A FLASH The very essence of the triune God is that he is truth; therefore, he cannot lie.

Numbers 23:19

God is not man, that *he should lie,*

also see Heb. 6:18

or a son of man, that he should

change his mind. Has he said, and

will he not do it? Or has he spoken,

and will he not fulfill it?

WHAT HE IS LIKE

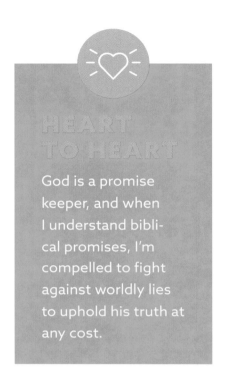

HEART TO HEART

God is a promise keeper, and when I understand biblical promises, I'm compelled to fight against worldly lies to uphold his truth at any cost.

God is a promise keeper, and he cannot lie (Titus 1:2). In working through *Flash Theology*, you're laying a foundation of God's character and truth, and placing his promises within your heart, mind, and soul. **Knowing God as a truth-teller gives us assurance to walk in authority and live with godly integrity as we trust that God is who he says he is.**

His promises are not casual, offhand remarks. They are rock-solid, set-in-stone commitments made by the truth-teller himself. We also read in 2 Peter 3:9 that "the Lord is not slow to fulfill his promise as some count slowness, but is patient toward you, not wishing that any should perish, but that all should reach repentance." God's promises will come to pass, but we must remain faithful and do our part as needed.

Some of God's promises are conditional, and others are unconditional. In other words, sometimes God's promises are based on our obedience, and other times they are not. **God's unconditional promises are not determined by us, but by the hope we have in Christ.** No stipulations or conditions are attached to these promises, and they're usually grace driven and benevolent in nature. For example, we hold on to the promise that Christ will come again (Heb. 9:27–28). Whether we accept or reject this truth, Christ is still coming!

There are also truths in the Bible that require us to ask or seek (see, for example, Matt. 7:7). It's a pattern to his promise that says, "If we keep our side of the promise, God will move on our behalf." We sometimes joke that those conditional promises are like making a pinky promise with God. To receive these promises, we must walk in God's will and ways and remain faithful.

PROMISES OF GOD

THE PROMISE	VERSE	REFERENCE
God's love is everlasting and never-ending.	For I am sure that neither death nor life, nor angels nor rulers, nor things present nor things to come, nor powers, nor height nor depth, nor anything else in all creation, will be able to separate us from the love of God in Christ Jesus our Lord.	Rom. 8:38–39
God provides for my needs and gives strength.	And the LORD will guide you continually and satisfy your desire in scorched places and make your bones strong; and you shall be like a watered garden, like a spring of water, whose waters do not fail.	Isa. 58:11
God is with me.	For he [Jesus] has said, "I will never leave you nor forsake you."	Heb. 13:5
God places the lonely in community.	God settles the solitary in a home; he leads out the prisoners to prosperity.	Ps. 68:6
God rescues me.	[Jesus says,] "The Spirit of the Lord is upon me, because he has anointed me to proclaim good news to the poor. He has sent me to proclaim liberty to the captives and recovering of sight to the blind, to set at liberty those who are oppressed, to proclaim the year of the Lord's favor."	Luke 4:18–19
God gave me Holy Spirit.	And it is God who establishes us with you in Christ, and has anointed us, and who has also put his seal on us and given us his Spirit in our hearts as a guarantee.	2 Cor. 1:21–22
God is my Father.	Father of the fatherless and protector of widows is God in his holy habitation.	Ps. 68:5
Jesus will come back.	And behold, I am coming soon.	Rev. 22:7

WHAT DOES THIS MEAN FOR ME?

Have you ever been in a relationship with someone who breaks their promises? It's hard to trust them. Don't let the lies of this world, or your lack of follow-through, distract you from the truth of God's Word and the authority of Scripture. Check out our website at flashtheology.com for a Promise Chart reminding you about some of the unconditional and conditional promises of God. We recognize there are thousands of life-giving promises found in Scripture; we are just highlighting a few.

Remember, what draws your attention molds you. Since all of God's promises find their yes in Christ (2 Cor. 1:20), as you give your attention to his promises, you're giving your attention to him.

APPLY THIS: Spend some time declaring God's promises during your prayer time today. Utilize the Promise Chart as you pray for yourself or others.

26

God Is Peace

IN A FLASH God establishes peace by means of the cross, ending the hostility we once had with him.

Isaiah 9:6

For to us a child is born, to us a

Prophetically pointing to Christ's birth

son is given; and the government

He will rule over everyone

shall be upon his shoulder, and his

name shall be called Wonderful

Counselor, Mighty God, Everlasting

Father, Prince of Peace.

Hebrew: Sar Shalom

WHAT HE IS LIKE

One of Jesus's most beloved titles is "Prince of Peace." However, the original Hebrew construction of the title, *Sar Shalom*, is a bit perplexing! Our English translation does not quite capture the tone of the original. A *sar* in Hebrew is not friendly, but has militaristic overtones, denoting a tyrant or warlord. A more precise translation might be "Warlord of Peace." How bizarre is that?

"Prince of Peace" certainly sounds better on a Christmas card than "Warlord of Peace." But what if this term, *warlord*, tells us something incredible about the character of God?

Almost a thousand years passed between the writing of Isaiah and the Gospels. Within that period, several transfers of power occurred—from Assyria to Babylon to Persia to Greece to, by the time Jesus was born, Rome. How did Rome come to power? Through brute force, military might, and political oppression on anyone who would challenge them. Rome even claimed to have established *pax Romana* ("Roman peace"), but had it? Was everyone truly experiencing the tranquility they were said to have established? Not a chance. The famous philosopher Epictetus—a contemporary of Luke—observed:

> While the emperor may give peace from war on land and sea, he is unable to give peace from passion, grief, and envy. He cannot give peace of heart, for which man yearns more than even for outward peace.[18]

Pax Romana was a political slogan, not a concrete reality. Part of the reason the Romans had not succeeded in bringing peace was that their methods of achieving and maintaining so-called peace were cruel and tyrannical. So the weary world waited for true peace to come. The world needed a Savior, the One who would truly bring peace.

Finally, "an angel of the Lord," quickly followed by "a multitude of the heavenly host" (Luke 2:9, 13), announced to some shepherds in a field that Jesus had been born. "Heavenly host" was a military term, a euphemism for an army. So heaven's army was deployed to announce the birth of the world's true king! The *Sar Shalom*, the "Warlord of Peace," had been born.

Here is where this gets especially odd. **Instead of coming as a bloodthirsty tyrant, Jesus was born with the very purpose to give his own blood to establish peace; something unprecedented from any ruler.**

And through him to reconcile

to himself all things,

whether on earth or in heaven,

making peace by the blood of his cross.

(COL. 1:20)

So Luke told of an army of heavenly angels announcing the birth of Jesus and singing a song about a peace offering from God. The paradox lies in the fact that the heavenly army was deployed for peace rather than war. Imagine a nation's military sending out their most highly trained men and women from all branches to invade a foreign land, but instead of bearing arms, they carry white flags symbolizing the invasion of peace into that land.

An invasion of peace? It sounds absurd, doesn't it? In the ancient world, no army had ever been deployed to bring peace before this army of angels. They came to proclaim that the holy, almighty God had brought down the white flag from heaven in the form of Jesus Christ.

Instead of coming with the armies of heaven to wage war against people, Jesus came with the purpose to wage war against sin, death, and the powers of darkness. **Christ did not wield a sword; he bore a cross. He did not shed the blood of others to establish peace; he shed his own blood.** This is good news; it is the gospel, and it communicates the heart of God.

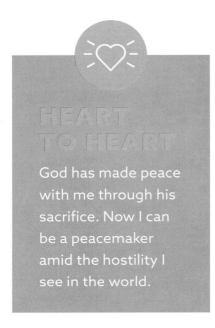

HEART TO HEART

God has made peace with me through his sacrifice. Now I can be a peacemaker amid the hostility I see in the world.

WHAT DOES THIS MEAN FOR ME?

For us, being part of "the Lord's army" (like the angels in Luke 2) means that we are called to be agents of peace, not war. That is how we follow in the footsteps of our king. Jesus emphasized this when he challenged his disciples to be "peacemakers" (Matt. 5:9). This is different from being a peacekeeper. Jesus had already secured the peace, but there was still work to be done. A weary world had yet to hear that the most important war had already been won. And because people did not know this, there was still hostility and unrest.

We receive the message of the gospel and then join the angels in announcing "Peace on earth!" The good news is something we announce to everyone, everywhere, beyond the Christmas season. True peace is very different from the Roman peace bought through military might. Our Prince of Peace (our *Sar Shalom*) secures the peace that our souls long for.

APPLY THIS: Reflect on your interactions in real life or online the past week. Were you being a peacebreaker, peacekeeper, or peacemaker?

27

God Is Happy

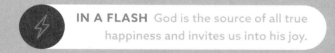

IN A FLASH God is the source of all true happiness and invites us into his joy.

Psalm 16:5-11

The LORD is my chosen portion

David is calling the Lord, not any other possession, his inheritance or his fortune.

and my cup; *you hold my lot.*

The lines have fallen for me in pleasant places; indeed, I have a beautiful inheritance. I bless the LORD who gives me counsel; in the night also my heart instructs me.

I have set the LORD always before me;

To keep all our senses captive and attentive to the Lord

because he is at my right hand, I shall not be shaken. Therefore _my heart is glad,_ and my whole being rejoices; my flesh also dwells secure. For you will not abandon my soul to Sheol, or let your holy one see

The realm of the dead is not our destiny.

corruption. You make known to me the path of life; in your presence there is fullness of joy; at your right

God's presence offers not partial or incomplete joy, but the fullness of joy.

hand are pleasures forevermore.

WHAT HE IS LIKE

We all have words, phrases, or sayings that make us cringe. For us, one of those is when someone says, "God doesn't want us to be happy; he wants us to be holy!" Eeeek! So cringeworthy. Here's why. This suggests that there is a fork in the road, with one way leading to *happiness* and the other leading to *holiness*. Do you see the problem? Is it not God who makes life vivid, colorful, and altogether wonderful? Is it not Satan and sin that rid life of what is truly good and beautiful?

Happiness and holiness are not two divergent paths; they are one path—and God is the pioneer of that path! It's when we blaze our own trail away from the "path of life" (Ps. 16:11) that we find a fraudulent and fleeting kind of happiness.

As Christians, we don't define happiness—or truth, justice, or love—the way the world does. There are more than fifteen Greek and Hebrew words that can be translated as "happy," and it seems this topic was important to the inspired writers of the Bible. When we study Scripture, words like *joy* and *happiness* are intertwined and overlap, because at times we have joy and happiness despite what's going on, or experience the joy and happiness of God as we relish the good.

KEY HEBREW AND GREEK NOUNS FOR HAPPINESS AND JOY

ORIGINAL WORD	EXAMPLE VERSES
Hebrew: *'ašrê*, "happy; blessed"	Ps. 1:1; 34:8; 41:1; 112:1; 128:1; Isa. 30:18
Hebrew: *śimḥâ*, "joy; delight; gladness"	Ps. 16:11; 21:6; Isa. 29:19; 35:10; 55:12; 61:7
Greek: *makarios*, "happy; blessed"	Matt. 5:3; Acts 20:35; Rom. 4:7; Rev. 22:14
Greek: *chara*, "joy; delight; great happiness"	Matt. 25:21; Luke 2:10; John 15:11; Rom. 15:13; Gal. 5:22

The prophet Zephaniah talked about both God's wild love for us and his warm delight in us: "The L ORD your God is with you, the Mighty Warrior who saves. He will take **great delight in you**; in his love he will no longer rebuke you, but will **rejoice over you** with singing" (Zeph. 3:17 NIV). Only a happy God could express such emotion. And to think that we, his runaway people, could be the object of his delight? It's almost too much to bear! But that's our God. Jesus even shared a parable to describe how he will respond to his disciples at his return as an invitation to "come and share your master's happiness" (Matt. 25:21, 23 NIV).

Charles Spurgeon found this to be a passion point of his preaching. Not only did he directly make a connection between holiness and happiness more than five hundred times in his preaching, but he also spoke of happiness thousands of times. Here is one thing he said:

> [Christians] should be happy, because they serve a happy God. It enters into the essential idea of God that he is superlatively blessed. We cannot conceive of a God who should be infinitely miserable. Our written rule and guide speaks of him whom we adore as "God over all, *blessed for ever.*" ... [W]hat, I believe, is an equally accurate translation, "the *happy* God." As it is true that "God is love," so is it equally true that *God is happiness*. Now it would be an exceedingly strange thing if, in proportion as we became like a happy God, we grew more and more miserable.[19]

Spurgeon's point is compelling. As we walk with God, do we become happier or more miserable? Reconsider Psalm 16:5–11. Maybe you need to highlight, circle, or underline the word *fullness* in verse 11. There is not partial or consolatory joy in the presence of God, but fullness of joy. Of course, this is meant to stoke our imagination and enthusiasm regarding when we, one day, will be face to face with God! But this is also meant to tell us about God's heart—his happy heart—and how we can relate to him and live differently in light of it.

WHAT DOES THIS MEAN FOR ME?

One of the reasons Israel was chastised was when they did not "serve the LORD your God with joyfulness and gladness of heart" (Deut. 28:47). God expects our service to him to be a delight, not a drudgery. Could this be because God knows that when we are not walking in his joy we are generally more susceptible to sin? By contrast, what happens when we do, indeed, serve the Lord with "joyfulness and gladness"? The book of Nehemiah sheds some insight on this.

Nehemiah tells the story of the exiled Israelites returning to Jerusalem to rebuild the city's broken walls. In leading them to restore the walls, God was also beginning to restore the people's identity as his covenant people. After much persistence and devotion, the walls were completed, and the people gathered to consecrate and rededicate themselves to the Lord.

HEART TO HEART

God wants me to be happy and holy, which comes by trusting his way toward this end.

> And Nehemiah, who was the governor, and Ezra the priest and scribe, and the Levites who taught the people said to all the people, "This day is holy to the LORD your God; do not mourn or weep." … Then he said to them, "Go your way. Eat the fat and drink sweet wine and send portions to anyone who has nothing ready, for this day is holy to our Lord. And do not be grieved, for the joy of the LORD is your strength." … And all the people went their way to eat and drink and to send portions and to make great rejoicing, because they had understood the words that were declared to them. (Neh. 8:9–10, 12)

When the faith of the covenant people was revived, their joy was restored as well. On such a monumental day for the people, they were forbidden from mourning or weeping (v. 9) and were told to go "eat the fat and drink sweet wine"—in essence, go party! **Revival and rejoicing go together! We can never underestimate the quality of worship that comes from a happy heart.** In this context, Nehemiah declares, "The joy of the LORD is your strength" (v. 10).

When God's people remember who they are called to be, and return to walking with God, joyful festivity and celebration are the natural response. After all, God is the author of the party. He commanded his people to practice the festivals (a.k.a., parties) that he gave to them. And Jesus often compared the kingdom of God to a great feast (see, for example, Matt. 22:1–14) and considered it condemning to deny the wonderful invitation.

Maybe we need to meditate more on the happy heart of God, who invites us to share in his happiness with him. Consider what Clement of Alexandria (AD 150–215) wrote: "All our life is like a day of *celebration* for us; we are convinced, in fact, that God is always everywhere. We work while singing, we sail while reciting hymns, we accomplish all other occupations of life while praying."[20] Coming from Clement of Alexandria, these are powerful words, considering he and his audience faced hostility and persecution. God's gift of happiness is not conditional on what is happening, but it is positional, rooted and secure in Christ.

What would happen if we saw life, as Clement did, as a "celebration," awaiting an even greater celebration when our King returns? Could the Christian's happiness be the key to a contagious faith?

APPLY THIS: How does our theology of happiness or joy invite us to treat life as a celebration? Practice intentional happiness today, and celebrate God in the process.

28

God
Is Wise

IN A FLASH God is omnisapient; his infinite wisdom
allows us to trust that he knows what he's doing.

Romans 16:25-27

Now to him who is able to
······· God

strengthen you *according to my*

gospel and the preaching of Jesus

Christ, according to the revelation

of the mystery that was kept secret

see 1 Cor. 2:7 ························

for long ages but has now been

disclosed and through the prophetic

writings has been made known to all nations, according to the command of the eternal God, to bring about the obedience of faith—to the only wise God be glory forevermore through Jesus Christ! Amen.

WHAT HE IS LIKE

A beautiful and notable thing about God is that he lacks nothing. He is not void of wisdom, nor will he ever run out. God's wisdom isn't attained or assimilated into his character; it is his character. It's one of those deep philosophical things we should ponder: How does God's wisdom impact us? If God truly is wise, why are mosquitoes ruining our lives? *(Perhaps mosquitoes are a result of the fall.)* And how do we see God's wisdom on display throughout the Bible? All great questions. Let's tackle a few.

God is omnisapient, a fancy Latin word meaning "all-wise." The apostle Paul described him as "the only wise God" (Rom. 16:27) in a letter he wrote to the Roman church around AD 57. The book of Romans is often considered one of the most systematic, precise representations of Christian doctrine in the Bible. Paul closed this important letter with a doxology (a liturgical expression praising God). He could have celebrated Christ as Savior or highlighted how he delivered us from sin, made us righteous, or any of the other key theological truths he wrote about in the letter. Instead, Paul affirmed Christ as the revealed Messiah and then glorified "the only wise God." We can't help but think of the deep significance of Paul's choice in concluding Romans in celebration of God's wisdom.

How do we define wisdom? **Wisdom is choosing the right way to achieve a desired outcome.** Wisdom takes form with knowledge. Knowledge is having familiarity and understanding of something. Wisdom applies knowledge, experience, skill, and truth to select the proper path or do the right thing. People often have knowledge without wisdom, but we cannot have wisdom without knowledge. But God is divine, both infinitely wise and knowledgeable. His wisdom will never stop, cease, or dissipate. It stands the test of time, and within his wisdom flows an unlimited amount of knowledge, comfort, and guidance.

Let's reflect on Job's story in the Old Testament. Job was in a season of suffering and deep sorrow. His friends blamed his hardships and heartache on his sin. Meanwhile, Job cried out to God for answers to the hard mysteries of life. God did not directly answer Job's questions or concerns. Instead, he asked Job a series of questions (Job 38–40), such as: "Who is this that darkens counsel by words without knowledge? … Where were you when I laid the foundation of the earth? … Do you know the ordinances of the heavens? Can you establish their rule on the earth? … Who has put wisdom in the inward parts or given understanding to the mind? Who can number the clouds by wisdom?" Reflecting on God's questions, we see that, as we get fixated on wondering why various things have happened, we display a lack of trust in God and his wisdom.

When you trust people are wise, you listen and do what they say, often without asking for further clarification. You know they are the masters of their domains, and they've proved that to you. They're the experts in the field. Verse after verse supports the truth that God is wise, Holy Spirit gives wisdom (1 Cor. 12:8–10), and Christ is wisdom embodied (1 Cor. 1:30; Col. 2:1–3).

We may *know* God is the master of our domain, but we often get in our own way of embracing him as Master. God knows what he is doing. He is infinite and sees the beginning from the end as well as the trajectory of your life and the world; we do not. **Trusting God means welcoming his mystery, majesty, and wisdom to override our whys and what-ifs as we walk in his ways, wisdom, and blessing.**

HEART TO HEART

God is infinite in wisdom, and he also gives us his wisdom so we can see things from his perspective.

WHAT DOES THIS MEAN FOR ME?

If we believe this statement to be true, "God is all-powerful, all-knowing, and all-wise," then we should effortlessly do what he says and align our lives to him and a worldview based on biblical morals and truth. So why do we often not? In that question, we're reminded of a quote from celebrated French-Dominican pastor J. M. L. Monsabré, who said, "If God would concede me his omnipotence for twenty-four hours, you would see how many changes I would make in the world. But if he gave me his wisdom too, I would leave things as they are."[21] Just marinate on that for a moment! We all could think of what we would do differently if we had God's infinite power. I can think of like five things I would have changed this week alone! But if we had God's wisdom, wouldn't we keep things on the trajectory they are going? It is important to note here that we are not saying God likes or condones all that is happening, but in his wisdom, his big plan is not being thwarted and will put things toward an ultimate end far greater than we could contrive!

Eve is a great example of this dilemma between power and wisdom. In her desire to be wise, she disobeyed God (Gen. 3:6). Our quest for knowledge and wisdom should be rooted in a desire not to become God, but to be his image bearers. There's a difference, namely that we become like him through a transformative relationship with him without taking his place as the King of the Universe. We understand our position in God's story. We are not in control of the universe, nor are we the hero of humanity, but within the intimacy of knowing our Creator, we have access to godly wisdom. From this place, we reflect him to the world around us.

James, a servant of God who wrote an epistle (letter) in the Bible, spoke about wisdom. The book of James is similar to the wisdom literature of Proverbs, urging God's people to act like God. The following passage describes two types of wisdom: harmful wisdom and hopeful wisdom. We'll stop sugarcoating this conversation; James refers to wisdom that is produced from either demonic qualities or divine qualities. We've also fully expanded on these types of wisdom in the illustrations below.

COMPARE DEMONIC AND DIVINE WISDOM

Who is wise and understanding among you? By his good conduct let him show his works in the meekness of wisdom. But if you have bitter jealousy and selfish ambition in your hearts, do not boast and be false to the truth. This is not the wisdom that comes down from above, but is earthly, unspiritual, demonic. For where jealousy and selfish ambition exist, there will be disorder and every vile practice. But the wisdom from above is first pure, then peaceable, gentle, open to reason, full of mercy and good fruits, impartial and sincere. And a harvest of righteousness is sown in peace by those who make peace. (James 3:13–18)

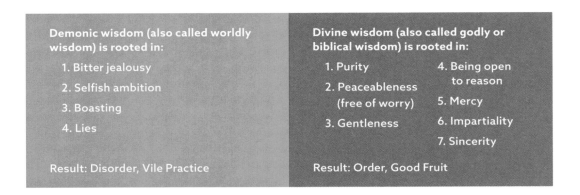

Demonic wisdom (also called worldly wisdom) is rooted in:	Divine wisdom (also called godly or biblical wisdom) is rooted in:	
1. Bitter jealousy	1. Purity	4. Being open to reason
2. Selfish ambition	2. Peaceableness (free of worry)	5. Mercy
3. Boasting		6. Impartiality
4. Lies	3. Gentleness	7. Sincerity
Result: Disorder, Vile Practice	Result: Order, Good Fruit	

You may be able to place yourself in either category of wisdom depending on the situation. In showcasing demonic wisdom, whether you realize it or not, you're partnering with the enemy's ways and helping him achieve his desired outcome. You know, that one social media post where you got super snarky, or you told that half-truth and ignored the conviction of Holy Spirit. Or perhaps you struggle with jealousy of a coworker or friend. Demonic wisdom can sneak in on you if you're unrepentant, not practicing spiritual disciplines regularly or spending time with the Lord.

What would it look like to truly walk in godly wisdom? You would be open to reason, overwhelmed with mercy, not discriminatory, and have pure and sincere intentions within your decision-making. It starts with understanding Job 28:28, that in fearing the Lord, there is wisdom. Proverbs 9:10 echoes those words, saying, "The fear of the LORD is the beginning of wisdom, and the knowledge of the Holy One is insight."

Both supernatural wisdom and knowledge are gifts from God, given to his people. Godly wisdom impacts the life of a believer through conviction and repentance and creates a desire toward godly transformation. We must trust God to provide the ability to make the right choices within our parenting, relationships, leadership, career and callings, and day-to-day tasks as we learn to walk in his will.

We pray God continues to provide supernatural wisdom for you—wisdom on when to speak and when to be still, when to push forward and when to pause, how to bravely take action and boldly share encouragement with others. You're not a fool, but a wise and godly leader who fears God and places him first. You know his plan is holy, just, purposed, and that he's positioning you for his best—and there's no better place to be.

APPLY THIS: Spend some time reviewing the two types of wisdom in the chart. Prayerfully consider and reflect on the ways you've placed God first and subsequently have gained wisdom in certain areas. Are there any areas where you lack wisdom and should repent and seek out God for help?

29

God Is Kind

Matthew 11:28-30

Come to me, all who labor and are heavy laden, and I will give you rest. Take my yoke *upon you, and learn*

.... A term for a disciple being joined to a rabbi

from me, for I am <u>gentle</u> and <u>lowly</u> in heart, and you will find rest *for*

Sabbath rest ....

your souls. For my yoke is easy,

Greek word for "kind" (chrēstos) ....

and my burden is light.

WHAT HE IS LIKE

Few passages give us an interior look at the heart of Jesus like Matthew 11:28–30. Our Lord reminds us that he is "gentle and lowly in heart." What could be more inviting? It is opposite how most people view the character of God.

Verses 29 and 30 mention the "yoke" Jesus offers. This is an agricultural metaphor as well as a metaphor of a student to his rabbi. Those who respond to the call of Jesus will "learn from" him (v. 29). Once yoked, the disciple's life is no longer isolated but cooperating, as their whole existence has transitioned into companionship. Perhaps the most surprising thing about these verses is that Jesus's yoke is described as "easy."

Of the seventeen uses of *chrēstos* ("kind") and *chrēstotēs* ("kindness") in Scripture, eleven of them refer to something belonging to or coming from God. Here are some examples:

ESV TRANSLATION: CHRĒSTOS ("KIND"), CHRĒSTOTĒS ("KINDNESS")	VERSE	REFERENCE
God's character is accredited to being kind.	But love your enemies, and do good, and lend, expecting nothing in return, and your reward will be great, and you will be sons of the Most High, for he is **kind** to the ungrateful and the evil.	Luke 6:35
God's kindness is a means to our salvation.	Or do you presume on the riches of his kindness and forbearance and patience, not knowing that God's **kindness** is meant to lead you to repentance?	Rom. 2:4
God's kindness is offered as an alternative to his severity.	Note then the **kindness** and the severity of God: severity toward those who have fallen, but God's **kindness** to you, provided you continue in his **kindness**. Otherwise you too will be cut off.	Rom. 11:22

ESV TRANSLATION: CHRĒSTOS ("KIND"), CHRĒSTOTĒS ("KINDNESS")	VERSE	REFERENCE
Kindness is a core attribute and defining feature of love. (Here the verbal form of "kindness," *chrēsteuomai*, is used.)	Love is patient and **kind**; love does not envy or boast; it is not arrogant.	1 Cor. 13:4
Kindness is a fruit and product of Holy Spirit at work in our lives.	But the fruit of the Spirit is love, joy, peace, patience, **kindness**, goodness, faithfulness, gentleness, self-control; against such things there is no law.	Gal. 5:22–23
God's grace toward us is a way in which his kindness will be on display for ages and ages to come.	So that in the coming ages he might show the immeasurable riches of his grace in **kindness** toward us in Christ Jesus.	Eph. 2:7

When we accept Jesus's yoke, we take on something that is usually considered strenuous but Jesus insists is *chrēstos*, which literally means "kind,"[22] and is often translated "easy." If Jesus's yoke is "easy," then how does his call to self-sacrifice and carrying one's cross (Matt. 16:24–26) make sense? But if by using the word *chrēstos* Jesus instead meant that his yoke is kind, good, or beneficial, then we are challenged to view his yoke differently. Alluding to C. S. Lewis's description of Aslan (Jesus, in Lewis's Chronicles of Narnia), Jesus is not safe, and his yoke is not always easy, but he is good and his yoke is always kind.

 FUN FACT

The Greek adjective *chrēstos* and related words have a wide semantic range of meaning, conveying ideas such as: "kind," "good," "useful," "beneficial," and "mild."

As followers of Jesus, we too are "yoked" to him. This means that we are joined or connected to him, like a side-by-side companion. But instead of being a burden, his yoke is a blessing. When we are hitched to his kind and good yoke, we see life through his eyes; it's like we finally start to see in color for the first time.

The yoke of Jesus is like balm on a blistered soul. **Jesus's yoke will ease the disciple who takes it on, but it will not always be an *easy* yoke to bear. It is light in weight but not void of any obligation.** Nevertheless, the emphatic gift to the one who responds to the call to "come" (Matt. 11:28) is one of "rest." The ease of the yoke all depends on who one is yoked to. Everyone is yoked to something; Jesus, however, offers a yoke that is beneficial and uplifting. Thus, Jesus presented himself as one who refreshes the weary and deals gently with those yoked to him—picking up those who find themselves too weary and burdened under their current yokes.

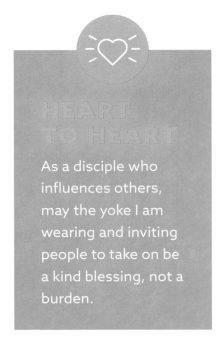

HEART TO HEART

As a disciple who influences others, may the yoke I am wearing and inviting people to take on be a kind blessing, not a burden.

Speaking of Matthew 16:24–26, where the disciples were challenged to carry their crosses, the seventeenth-century Scottish theologian Samuel Rutherford wrote, "His cross is the sweetest burden that ever I bare; it is such a burden as wings are to a bird, or sails are to a ship, to carry me forward to my harbour."[23] Jesus accompanies and leads us out of a "gentle and lowly" heart (Matt. 11:29). The yoke is normally a symbol of labor. But Jesus's yoke of rest and ease typified the rest of messianic redemption as promised by the Sabbath.

WHAT DOES THIS MEAN FOR ME?

If we are honest, it is usually easier to act with conviction than with kindness. Being kind can be costly, as it often means being more even-tempered than the people we deal with or the situations we find ourselves in. **But what would happen if we were the kindest people to be around? Especially for those who are yoked to us in a variety of ways—family members, colleagues, friends—do they experience a kind yoke with us?** Would they say we bring a steady ease to their lives? Or are we just another one of the many who make life harder than it should be? These are serious questions for us to consider and reflect on. After all, we represent Christ. The title "Christian" is not just something given to us by coincidence; it's a high honor. May we live honorably by reflecting the immense kindness of Christ into our world.

APPLY THIS: One way you can remain yoked to Jesus is through fasting. Biblical fasting is when you temporarily give up something, whether a meal, media, or something else you love, and turn your full attention to Jesus instead. Try fasting with the soul desire for more of God and a deeper hunger for his kindness to be reflected within your life!

30

God Is Glorious

IN A FLASH God's glory is a manifestation of his salvation, presence, and beauty.

Psalm 19:1-4 (NIV)

The heavens declare the glory of God;

In Hebrew, the verb for "declare" is an intensive action. The proclamation is not bland or even tame; it is a vigorous expression of worship!

the skies proclaim the work of his hands.

Day after day they pour forth speech;

night after night they reveal knowledge.

They have no speech, they use no words;

no sound is heard from them. Yet their

voice goes out into all the earth, their

words to the ends of the world.

WHAT HE IS LIKE

God is glorious. No one disputes it, but few seem to understand what it means. So what is God's glory about anyway? To answer, we have to see God's glory through three distinct lenses.

FUN FACT

The Hebrew word for "glory," *kavod*, primarily means "weight," referring to something being substantial and significant.

God's glory is the manifestation of his salvation. Exodus 15 is peppered with various Hebrew translated as "gloriously" and "majesty" to describe God's saving power over the Egyptians. Here, God's glory colors the quality of power God has—it is far above and beyond all else! Likewise, Paul's great eulogy in Ephesians 1:3–14 shows us that part of the purpose of God's saving plan is to bring him glory (vv. 6, 12, 14). We give glory to God by declaring how great he is, since a key aspect of his glory is how it is revealed in our rescue. And let's be real: we cannot add to God's glory; we can only magnify it.

God's glory is a manifestation of his presence. Often in Scripture, the word *glory* is used in tandem with an exhibition of God's powerful presence (such as in Ex. 16; 24; Lev. 9; Deut. 5:24; John 1:14; Heb. 1:3; 1 Pet. 4:14). In the first eight chapters of Leviticus, God prepared the Israelites for something big, utilizing rituals and ceremonial practices that would speak to *them* in *their* day and context. Finally, in chapter 9, we see what it is all about:

> Then Moses and Aaron went into the Tabernacle, and when they came back out, they blessed the people again, and **the glory of the LORD appeared to the whole community**. Fire blazed forth from the LORD's

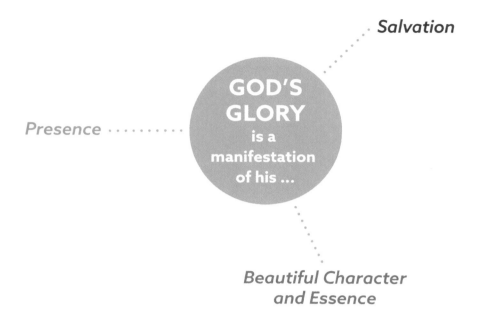

presence and consumed the burnt offering and the fat on the altar. When the people saw this, they shouted with joy and fell face down on the ground. (vv. 23–24 NLT)

Ah! So everything God had his people do was to prepare them for a glorious encounter with him. The Lord manifested himself with fire and consumed the offerings, leaving people beyond a state of coherent words. All they could do was shout and fall down in awe and worship. God's glory was a means to show himself to people through a majestic display of his power. This is something that can happen today as we press into the presence of God. We can posture ourselves in awe of the Lord of glory, whether corporately or in solitude, and in return we can experience a powerful moment where he overwhelms us with a manifestation of his presence.

God's glory is a manifestation of his beautiful character and essence. Most of us probably grasp that God's character is beautiful. But God's beauty is more than what he does; it is what he is. Isaiah's vision of the messianic King said, "Your eyes will behold the king in his beauty" (Isa. 33:17), highlighting the awe of our God's glorious appearance. If we saw his uncovered beauty (as we one day will!), it would take our breath away. We worship a beautiful God, whose beauty stokes our worship even brighter.

We think of creation as beautiful, but does that not simply reflect the beauty of the Creator? God is beautiful (1 Chron. 16:27; Ps. 27:4; 96:6; 104:1–2; 113:4; Isa. 33:17), and God's creation reflects his beauty (Ps. 8:1; 19:1–2; Isa. 6:3; Hab. 2:14; Rom. 1:20). There is something special about being with God in nature, and it's often a great way to connect with him! **Enjoying God in his creation is like enjoying the company of an artist in the midst of his gallery.** So don't be afraid to get outdoors and marvel at the majesty of our glorious God!

HEART TO HEART

God's glory is all-encompassing, making everything we do an opportunity to glorify him.

WHAT DOES THIS MEAN FOR ME?

Every night a sermon is being preached—365 days a year! Do you hear it? It's the sermon of the stars. And the endless specs of light in the sky are declaring God's glory and craftsmanship. They do so without saying a single word, yet their message is heard from every point of the globe (Ps. 19:1–4). How can this be? Because God's glory can be seen, heard, and experienced even beyond the ways in which he dramatically interacts in our lives. It's like we forget that the original greatest miracle was the moment when God made everything from nothing.

Ever since their genesis, the starry skies have never stopped announcing the story of the glory of the Creator God. No matter where you are, you cannot escape their song. You can shut your spiritual eyes and cover your ears to their worship, but you cannot hinder their praise. You will find that the grandeur of creation is only the springboard, the catalyst, as it propels your soul to soar in worship.

One of the best things you can do for your soul is to allow yourself to feel *small* and allow the ever-expanding galaxies to make you reflect on how *big* God is. Feeling small is not belittling but empowering when you know you are in the loving hands of the Master of the Universe. That sense of awe is one of the most enlivening feelings. After all, few things fight our *worries* like comparing them to the *wonder* of how big our God is!

The stars aren't just preaching; they're singing! Do you hear their symphony of praise? They beckon you to join their song in magnifying the glory of our God!

The heavens declare the glory of God;

    the skies proclaim the work of his hands.

Day after day they pour forth speech;

    night after night they reveal knowledge.

They have no speech, they use no words;

    no sound is heard from them.

Yet their voice goes out into all the earth,

    their words to the ends of the world.

In the heavens God has pitched a tent for the sun.

(PS. 19:1–4 NIV)

APPLY THIS: Next time there are clear night skies, get outside and gaze at the glory of the stars (bonus points if you can get a view with less light pollution). Enjoy the silent but strong message as the stars declare God's glory. Feel small for a while, and allow God to give you a sense of how big he is.

31

God Is
Sabbath Rest

IN A FLASH God's heart is at ease and provides Sabbath rest through his relational presence.

Genesis 2:1-3

Thus the heavens and the

completed/accomplished ┄┄┄┄

earth were finished, and all the host

┄┄┄ *also see John 19:28–30*

of them. And on the seventh day

God finished his work that he

had done, and he rested on the

šāḇaṯ, ceased from all activity/observe the Sabbath ┄┄┄

seventh day from all his work that

he had done. So God blessed

Exodus 20:8–11

set apart/consecrated

the seventh day and made it holy,

because on it God rested

from all his work that he had

done in creation.

Any parent can tell you that rest is vital for a child's health. Without it, children become cranky, overwhelmed, and ride the struggle bus. Often parents will schedule their day around nap time, create sacred space for their baby to sleep, and soothe the child with lullabies and night-lights. Helping a son or daughter rest isn't something parents do out of obligation, but something they do because it's within their nature to love and care for their child.

WHAT GOD IS LIKE

Here we lie, tossing and turning, haunted by the tension of our own broken humanity filled with chaos, sin, and sorrow. Similar to a healthy parent-child relationship, God helps us find rest. In fact, his divine nature embodies rest. He cares so deeply for our well-being that he created a way to bring his rest to our restless souls. God not only made a way for us to rest through relationship with him, but as loving fathers do, he also leads by example.

Rest at Creation

The beginning of the Bible kicks off with God creatively working. As Holy Spirit hovered, God spoke and separated light from the darkness and brought order to the chaos (Gen. 1:1–4). Like a master painter setting down his brush, God then exclaimed, "It is finished" (at least for now!).

God rested. He set apart one day within his workweek and stopped to behold the beauty of the work he had done. This became known as Sabbath rest, an intentional time to cease from all creative activity to presently enjoy what has been made. God set up a pattern that he later commanded the Israelites to obey.

Exodus 20:8 shares the fourth commandment, which reads, "Remember the Sabbath day, to keep it holy." Sabbath became known as a foretaste of eternity itself. It's a sacred day when we stop working *on* life to enter in and be present with the life that surrounds us.

It is both a practical work we enter into and a spiritual work God brings about. Sabbath is both absence and presence. For example, it is the absence of the toil and struggle of your workweek and a pause of the pressure you may feel to perform. Sabbath gives you a full day to stop working and to simply enjoy God, his provision, his creation, and his people. God created this sacred rhythm to create a healthier you! It's so much more than simply a day off or sneaking away for nap time to escape life's realities. It's resting from the toil of life to enjoy the deeper meaning of life!

Rest at the Cross

True Sabbath rest stems from the very heart of Jesus. In Matthew 11:28, Jesus called out, "Come to me, all who labor and are heavy laden, and I will give you [Sabbath] rest." The rest we long for is found in him and no one else. It is a gift received by grace. It's found through God's gift of salvation, which invites us into a relationship with God himself. A relationship that was built from the love of a Father who gave his one and only Son so that our souls could find rest. Sin kept our souls in a perpetual state of restlessness—never satisfied, always searching in all the wrong places. But the cross brings us to God, where we join him in a state of soul rest and live our lives from that newfound state of being, which stems from the very heart of our Lord.

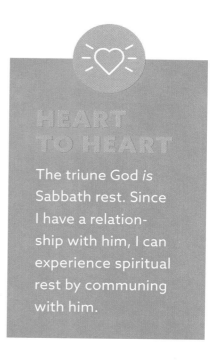

HEART TO HEART

The triune God *is* Sabbath rest. Since I have a relationship with him, I can experience spiritual rest by communing with him.

Rest in the New Creation

God has given us Sabbath rest right now, and it's also something we can look forward to within its fullness. Although we have begun to taste the effects of God's rest through the power and residence of Holy Spirit, like an appetizer leading to the main course, the best rest is yet to come.

WHAT DOES THIS MEAN FOR ME?

Slavery is the opposite of Sabbath; slavery to twelve-hour workdays, fearing the bogey-man in the nighttime hours, or shame from the past that causes us to separate from God in the present. Rest brings a break from worldly striving and settles our souls. We Sabbath because we are free.

We Sabbath not only to fulfill a spiritual discipline but also because it is the greatest expression of eternity and oneness with Christ. It's a sign and benefit of being in a covenant relationship with him.

As we understand God's Sabbath rest, we begin to commune in the way he's created for us. Scripture shares that "God's promise of entering his rest still stands, so we ought to tremble with fear that some of you might fail to experience it" (Heb. 4:1 NLT). This is the promised rest we have by being his child. It's a rest we get to actively receive from a caring Father. Again, it's both practical and spiritual.

How is your schedule set apart for Sabbath? God asks us to "remember Sabbath" (Deut. 5:12 CSB), because when we forget the meaning of Sabbath, we forget the bigger picture of what he's doing in liberating the world. Yet many of us say, "I'm busy," as if it were a badge of honor. Busyness is not a divine quality, but a demonic one. If you find yourself too busy for Sabbath, you are busier than God. To truly understand and experience Sabbath rest, we need to experience freedom. We must give God sacred space within our calendars. And when we do, we discover it is so worth it!

As God declared a work finished in creation, a work was finished at the cross, and the final work will be finished when Jesus returns to earth. That word "finished" is a lexical link connecting to Sabbath rest. Chaos, sin, and sorrow cease as we find rest dwelling in the presence of Christ.

FUN FACT

A lexical link is when a specific word is used in a way that shows biblical parallels observed.

SABBATH REST

TRADITIONAL SABBATH Rest at Creation	TRIUMPHANT SABBATH Rest at the Cross	TIMELESS & TRUE SABBATH Rest in the New Creation

YOU ARE HERE (rough estimate)

Chaos was brought into order within creation; Sabbath rest is found in the practice of biblical time management.	Sin was conquered with Jesus's sacrificial death on the cross; Sabbath rest is given to those who trust him.	Sorrow is ended as Jesus returns; Sabbath rest is truly found as God comes home to be with his people.
So the creation of the heavens and the earth and everything in them was completed. On the seventh day God had **finished** his work of creation, so he rested from all his work. Genesis 2:1–2 (NLT)	When Jesus had tasted it, he said, "It is **finished**!" Then he bowed his head and gave up his spirit. It was the day of preparation, and the Jewish leaders didn't want the bodies hanging there the next day, which was the Sabbath (and a very special Sabbath, because it was Passover week). John 19:30–31 (NLT)	And the one sitting on the throne said, "Look, I am making everything new!" And then he said to me, "Write this down, for what I tell you is trustworthy and true." And he also said, "It is **finished**! I am the Alpha and the Omega—the Beginning and the End. To all who are thirsty I will give freely from the springs of the water of life." Revelation 21:5–6 (NLT)

We're living in the already-and-not-yet tension, where God's kingdom already resides on earth but not yet in the fullness of what it will be. Sabbath rest is thus impossible to fully receive as we live in this in-between. For now, we work, wait, and catch glimpses of all the good God is creating. And as we make time for him, we recognize he is already there.

The Sabbath is a commandment to rest and a covenant relationship where real rest resides. What future hope we have as Christ fully redeems a world of brokenness, disease, and distraction from himself! A place where creation and Christ followers are made whole, living free and inhabiting true Sabbath rest forever! Where chaos is brought to order and God is home among his people! May we see Christ face to face in the fullness of his eternal rest and welcome the day when he says, "It is finished!" Rest now in light of this assurance.

APPLY THIS: Get your calendar out right now, whether on your phone or a physical calendar, and schedule what day you will practice a traditional Sabbath. Discern what parameters will be helpful for you to detach from work and chores, and remember, the purpose is to enjoy life with God and others. Plan something relaxing or rejuvenating that day, and celebrate the goodness of God!

A Liturgy for Theologians

Dear God,

In a quest for knowledge, may
you quench our thirst with your
presence. Thank you for your holy
and sacred Word. May you use it to
shape our minds to be like yours.
Set our feet in motion toward you.
Brand our hearts by your love. And
bind our spirits to be one with you.
Amen, let it be.

Promises of God

Visit flashtheology.com for a downloadable Promises of God chart—see a short sample below and a portion of the larger chart in chapter 25. In the space underneath the sample, or on the full downloadable chart, feel free to add more biblical promises or write your own!

GOD IS FAITHFUL AND LOVING	VERSE	REFERENCE
God's Word is everlasting.	Heaven and earth will pass away, but my words will not pass away.	Mark 13:31
God is almighty.	With man it is impossible, but not with God. For all things are possible with God.	Mark 10:27
God is always faithful.	God is faithful, and he will not let you be tempted beyond your ability, but with the temptation he will also provide the way of escape, that you may be able to endure it.	1 Cor. 10:13

FIND MORE ON FLASHTHEOLOGY.COM!

For free resources geared toward personal devotion or group discussion, and for downloadable church materials, visit flashtheology.com.

 8-week small group guide for *Flash Theology*

> *Dig into scriptural truths, discover more about the whole person of God, and laugh and enjoy your time in a study group together, while maybe learning a thing or two along the way.*

 Church resources

> *Through a series of colorful slides, present to your church the key messages from Flash Theology that are rooted in Scripture.*

 Promises of God chart

> *Read some unconditional and conditional promises God makes to us throughout the Bible—how he is faithful and loving and how he offers us strength, wisdom, freedom, and hope.*

 Flash cards

> *Learn some of the key words in theological vocabulary, and test yourself and your friends.*

Visit flashtheology.com to also connect with the authors or invite Jenny and Brayden to speak at your event!

Take the next step and tell a friend or family member (or a complete stranger!) about what you've learned about God through *Flash Theology*.

Notes

1. A. W. Tozer, *The Knowledge of the Holy* (New York: HarperCollins, 1978), 1.

2. Brayden Brookshier, *A Resurrected Cosmos* (Dallas: Fontes Press, 2023).

3. καταναλίσκω (*katanaliskō*): "to destroy completely," Johannes P. Louw and Eugene Albert Nida, *Greek-English Lexicon of the New Testament: Based on Semantic Domains* (New York: United Bible Societies, 1996), 233.

4. William Arndt et al., *A Greek-English Lexicon of the New Testament and Other Early Christian Literature* (Chicago: University of Chicago Press, 2000), 11.

5. C. H. Spurgeon, *Morning and Evening: Daily Readings* (London: Passmore & Alabaster, 1896), July 15 morning reading.

6. Louw and Nida, *Greek-English Lexicon*, 384.

7. For Matthew, *proskyneō* ("to worship") favors the idea of worship, the kind of worship you ascribe to deity. See especially Matthew 28:9, 17 in the context of Jesus's resurrection and public exaltation as the king who now has received all authority in heaven and on earth (28:18), leaving no room for anyone to be outside his jurisdiction of kingship.

8. Jessica Lea, "The Surprising History behind 'Joy to the World,'" ChurchLeaders.com, December 23, 2019, https://churchleaders.com/worship/worship-videos/367481-surprising-history-joy-to-the-world.html.

9. John Stott, *Basic Christianity* (Nottingham, UK: Inter-Varsity Press, 2008), 173.

10. Chris Byrley, "Healing," in Douglas Mangum et al., eds., *Lexham Theological Wordbook* (Bellingham, WA: Lexham Press, 2014).

11. "Matthew's historical present places emphasis upon Jesus' command ... and perhaps more readily encourages the reader to apply the following words to himself." W. D. Davies and Dale C. Allison Jr., *A Critical and Exegetical Commentary on the Gospel according to Saint Matthew*, vol. 1, International Critical Commentary (London: T&T Clark International, 2004), 397.

12. C. H. Spurgeon, *My Sermon Notes: Matthew to Revelation*, vol. 3 (Bellingham, WA: Logos Bible Software, 2009), 396.

13. Darius Cikanavicius, "How Lack of Love in Childhood Robs Us of Love in Adulthood," Psych Central, September 30, 2019, https://psychcentral.com/blog/psychology-self/2019/09/trauma-lack-of-love#3.

14. JoAnna M. Hoyt, *Amos, Jonah, and Micah*, ed. H. Wayne House and William D. Barrick, Evangelical Exegetical Commentary (Bellingham, WA: Lexham Press, 2018), 809.

15. C. H. Spurgeon, "From Death to Life," in *The Metropolitan Tabernacle Pulpit Sermons*, vol. 9 (London: Passmore & Alabaster, 1863), 441.

16. Tom Wright, *Paul for Everyone: Galatians and Thessalonians* (London: Society for Promoting Christian Knowledge, 2004), 143.

17. Jack Zenger and Joseph Folkman, "What Great Listeners Actually Do," *Harvard Business Review*, July 14, 2016, https://hbr.org/2016/07/what-great-listeners-actually-do.

18. Epictetus, as quoted in Daniel M. Doriani, Philip Graham Ryken, and Richard D. Phillips, *The Incarnation in the Gospels*, Reformed Expository Commentary (Phillipsburg, NJ: P&R Publishing, 2008), 111.

19. C. H. Spurgeon, *The Sword and Trowel* (London: Passmore & Alabaster, 1866), 185.

20. Clement of Alexandria, quoted in "Historical Quotes," *Christianity Today*, accessed May 2, 2022, www.christianitytoday.com/history/quotes/.

21. Monsabré (1827–1907) is accepted as the source of this quote, which is likely from his preaching; though, it was never something he published in written form.

22. "The word group is used with ref. to God or Christ a few times. Jesus' claim that his yoke is χρηστός (along with 'my burden is light,' Matt 11:30) clearly means that what he expects of his disciples is not something onerous and will not make them weary … But the more fundamental point is that Jesus himself is 'gentle and humble in heart' … Moreover, in experiencing his gentleness, his disciples are to be like him by showing kindness to others ('learn from me,' 11:29a)." Moisés Silva, ed., *New International Dictionary of New Testament Theology and Exegesis*, vol. 4 (Grand Rapids, MI: Zondervan, 2014), 687.

23. Samuel Rutherford and Andrew A. Bonar, *Letters of Samuel Rutherford: With a Sketch of His Life and Biographical Notices of His Correspondents* (Edinburgh: Oliphant, Anderson & Ferrier, 1891), 262.

Acknowledgments

God has graced us to write words that, in the process, have fostered a deeper connection with himself. It's a humbling experience led with conviction and connection, and we are forever grateful to be led by his love. Ministry is a family job, and we've experienced that during the creation of *Flash Theology*. Thank you to our spouses, **Matt Randle** and **Ariana Brookshier**, who carved out space to support this calling through your time, prayers, and encouragement. Thank you to our crew of kids, **Max and Zoey Randle**, and **Kairo Brookshier**, for teaching us about child-like faith. Thank you to our **family** and **close friends** who prayed us through and often uncovered some of these theological truths beside us.

We are grateful for our team of publishing professionals who affirm and encourage us to show up when we often want to give up. **Steve Laube**, through your kindness, wisdom, and support with our first coauthored project, you turned our potential and passions into printed words. Thank you for laboring with us and representing us to this publishing world. **Michael Covington**, thank you for dreaming into this project, loving your authors well, and being a champion for Christ-centered resources within the church. You are a leader of leaders. And to the rest of the publishing team at **David C Cook**, who creates Flash Mob team names and welcomes us like family, your creativity and commitment to resourcing the Christian community is inspiring. The full Flash Mob includes: **Michael Covington**, **Stephanie Bennett**, **Kevin Scott**, **Jack Campbell**, **Katie Long**, **Rebecca Howard**, and **Annette Brickbealer**. And a super-special shout-out to **James Hershberger** for your art direction and inspiring the design team, **Micah Kandros** and **Emily Weigel**, to bring these theological concepts to life.

To our **pastors** and **church leaders**, thank you for your pastoral counsel and biblical teaching. You've shaped our theology through your love and leadership within our individual lives. Thank you to the Freedom Creatives ministry team, **Lonette Baity**, **Monique Leendertz-Lang**, and **Marie Horstdaniel**. To our **past and present church families**, your prayers and support are invaluable to us. And to **you**, dear reader, thank you for making yourself available to know and enjoy God more.

About the Authors

Brayden Brookshier and Jenny Randle are "framily" members (friends who are family). For over ten years, they've both served in ministry, developing resources that merge gospel-centered truths with practical application. Together, they love helping others learn all about the Christian faith ... in a flash. To find further resources, connect with the authors, or invite Brayden and Jenny to speak at your event, visit **flashtheology.com**.

Brayden Brookshier holds an MA in New Testament Research (Johnson University) and a BA in Biblical Studies (Horizon University), with both including an emphasis on biblical Greek exegesis. His passion is to help people feel the wonder and adventure of knowing God by taking people into an exploration of Scripture, like a time-traveling tour guide. He is the author of *A Resurrected Cosmos* (Fontes Press, 2023) and has participated as the theological editor for more than ten published books. He is a minister on staff with Newbreak Church (San Diego, CA) where he serves on the teaching team. Brayden also is the professor of biblical Greek at Horizon University. Brayden is a proud husband to Ariana and father to his son, Kairo. Listen to his podcast, *Adventures in Theology*.

Jenny Randle is an Emmy®-award-winning editor who went on a journey to discover what it really means to live on purpose. From a career in the heart of Hollywood to a Bible teacher, her creative ventures over the last twenty years have reached millions. In early 2018, Jenny and her husband, Matt, formed Freedom Creatives, a ministry organization that helps people live on purpose for the glory of God and good of others. Jenny is the author of *Courageous Creative*, *Getting to Know God's Voice*, and her newest book, *Dream Come True* (Harvest House Publishers). Jenny is currently working toward a master's in theology at Asbury Theological Seminary. Jenny and Matt live on an island in northern Florida with their two kids, Max and Zoey.

Find Brayden on Instagram: @braydenbrookshier
Jenny on Instagram: @jenny.randle